BEER

Facts, Figures & Fun

*"Any book without a mistake in it has had
too much money spent on it"*
Sir William Collins, publisher

BEER

Facts, Figures & Fun

Paul Barnett

Beer
Facts, Figures & Fun

Published by
Facts, Figures & Fun, an imprint of
AAPPL Artists' and Photographers' Press Ltd.
10 Hillside, London SW19 4NH, UK
info@ffnf.co.uk www.ffnf.co.uk
info@aappl.com www.aappl.com

Sales and Distribution
UK and export: Turnaround Publisher Services Ltd.
orders@turnaround-uk.com
USA and Canada: Sterling Publishing Inc. sales@sterlingpub.com
Australia & New Zealand: Peribo Pty. peribomec@bigpond.com
South Africa: Trinity Books. trinity@iafrica.com

A catalogue record for this book is available from the
British Library.

ISBN 13: 9781904332343
ISBN 10: 190433234X

Design (contents and cover): Malcolm Couch
mal.couch@blueyonder.co.uk

Printed in China by Imago Publishing
info@imago.co.uk

For information about custom editions, special sales, premium and
corporate purchases, please contact ffnf Special Sales
+44 20 8971 2094 or info@ffnf.co.uk

CONTENTS

INTRODUCTION: NOT JUST FROTH 7

BEER: A POTTED HISTORY 9

THE BREWS REVIVAL 31

ALL SORTS AND CONDITIONS OF BEER 35

Ale Types – Lager Types
Hybrid Types – Assorted Brews

A BEER CHARIVARI 53

Strange Brews – Not Just a Pretty Drink

THE PHANTOM BEERDRINKER:

URBAN LEGENDS 68

BEER "COCKTAILS" 71

FESTIVALS OF BEER 77

Some Notable Beer Festivals – Beer Festival Calendar

KEEP WATCHING THE BARS: BEER AWARDS 85

The Rate Beer Awards

The Australian International Beer Awards

The CAMRA Awards

Imbibliography

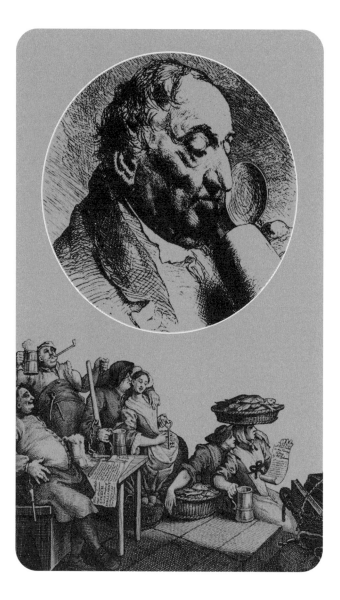

INTRODUCTION: NOT JUST FROTH

Through much of the 19th and 20th centuries, beer was held in low esteem throughout most of the English-speaking world. You could be a wine sophisticate, or a connoisseur of Scotch or brandy, but beer? Beer was just the stuff the commoners drank too much of in the pub on a Friday or Saturday night. It would be tempting to blame the Victorians for this sorry attitude, but Prince Albert was a good German and so presumably enjoyed his pint as much as the next man – and, of course, Victoria pointedly shared Albert's tastes, especially after he died, and transferred them on to her loyal subjects. Whatever the reason for beer's undervaluation, around the end of the last century's third quarter there was a renaissance in beer's reputation, a revolution started among the people and eventually shaking the pillars of the large breweries that had for far too long complacently subscribed to the common theory that beer was just "product", its consumers people of no discrimination upon whom virtually anything could be foisted. The result has been a return of beer at least some way to its former status as the drink of kings.

Talking of those kings, it's hard to appreciate quite how much beer was consumed by our ancestors. In large part this was because, in eras when hygiene was poorly understood, beer was a lot safer than water as a regular drink. Even so, it's hard to escape the conclusion that our ancestors must have spent much of their time severely smashed. Perhaps this might explain why humans have throughout history behaved with such stomach-churning savagery toward each other – just think for example of the sadism of the executions our forefathers not only tolerated as part of supposedly civilized society but also went in their throngs to witness. Empathy for one's fellow human can be an early casualty of intoxication. Likewise, a man is much more likely to declare war on whim when nursing a hangover . . .

There is obviously a whole new thesis of history to be written here, one that relates events not to religious movements or social changes but merely to the average level of intoxication in different regions at different times. Remember, you read it here first, even though you will not find a full exposition within these pages. Instead you will find the printed equivalent of an evening's good conversation in the tavern of your choice, as well as explanations of some of those beer-related facts and terms that you've heard the self-styled experts refer to so airily but which may have baffled you as much as they baffle any other normal human being.

So sit here in the corner where it's cozy, as far as you can possibly get from the jukebox without finding yourself in the carpark or the mensroom, make sure the glass in front of you is full, and . . .

BEER:
A POTTEDHISTORY

The art of making beer is at least 6000 years old. The first culture known for certain to have brewed beer extensively were the Sumerians, beginning some 6000 years ago. They brewed their beer from *bappir*, a type of unbaked bread dough made using the grain called emmer.

THE HYMN OF NINKASI

The ancient Sumerian goddess of brewing was Ninkasi, a complete hymn to whom survives on a tablet dated 1800BC. In part the hymn reads:

*Ninkasi, you are the one who waters the malt
set on the ground.
The noble dogs keep away even the potentates.*

*Ninkasi, you are the one who soaks the malt in a jar.
The waves rise, the waves fall.*

*Ninkasi, you are the one who spreads the cooked
mash on large reed mats.
Coolness triumphs.*

*Ninkasi, you are the one who holds with both
hands the great sweet wort.
Brewing with honey wine.*

*Ninkasi, when you pour out the filtered beer of the vat
It is like the flow of the Tigris and Euphrates.*

Also in the Sumerian pantheon was the god Dumuzi, one of whose special concerns was brewing.

Archaeologists have speculated that the art of making beer may in fact be far, far older than this – indeed, that our ancestors learned to brew beer before they learned to make bread. The cultivation of grain dates back nearly 10,000 years, and it is possible the grains were intended for brewing: in hot, moist climates, unleavened bread moulds very quickly, while fermented items last much longer. The discovery of beer may have come about when grain that had been stored too long eventually fermented.

In the Epic of Gilgamesh there are various references to beer, which was regarded alongside bread as the staff of life . In one tale, Gilgamesh sends a prostitute to find out more about his potential foe, the beast-man Enkidu: "Enkidu did not know what bread was, nor how one ate it. He had also not learned to drink beer. The prostitute said to Enkidu: 'Eat bread now, o Enkidu, as it belongs to life. Drink also beer, as it is the custom of the land.'" Enkidu does as she's told him and, after seven cups of beer, is so lifted in spirit that he bathes himself, the first step toward his acquisition of full humanity.

The Chinese god of alcohol is Yi–Ti (or Yi–Di). At the behest of the daughter of the Emperor Yu (23rd century BC), he created the most divine rice beer. The emperor pronounced it truly delicious, but reckoned it was far too strong: if people, emperors included, made a practice of drinking it, the fabric of society might unravel. He therefore forbade Yi–Ti from making any more. Yi–Ti did, though.

"Beer . . . a high and mighty liquor."
Julius Caesar

In *c*1116BC there appeared a Chinese imperial decree stating that the heavenly powers demanded people should take alcohol regularly and in moderation.

According to Robert Best, in his book *Noah's Ark and the Ziusudra Epic* (1999), the legendary Ark in which Noah saved all the animals of the world from the Deluge was in fact a beer, livestock and grain barge on the Euphrates River, with Noah himself being a king of the Sumerian city Shuruppak in about 2900BC. Six days of rainstorms caused the Euphrates to overflow its banks, and Noah took refuge on one of his barges. As the legend was passed down orally, successive tellers started exaggerating a bit . . .

The Babylonians learned the art of brewing from the Sumerians, and it is known they brewed at least twenty types of beer – eight from emmer, eight from barley, and four using a mixture of the two grains. They also exported beer to Egypt.

The Code of Hammurabi, dating from the 18th century BC, defined harsh penalties – death by drowning – for tavern-keepers who overcharged for their beer, served low-quality beer, or failed to report the presence of criminals in their taverns. The Code also set a daily beer ration: for ordinary workers it was about two litres, for civil servants about three litres, and for high priests about five litres. (Interesting that the ration for those who toiled all day in the hot sun was less than half that for the priests who could stay in their shady temples!)

The ancient Sumerians and Babylonians drank their beer through straws, to avoid swallowing the grain hulls still present in the beer. These straws are often shown alongside beer vessels on Sumerian seals and urns. Sir Leonard Woolley, during his excavations at Ur, found beer-drinking straws made of gold and lapis lazuli in the tomb of Lady Pu-abi.

ANCIENT AND MODERN

One of the odder brews was made in 1989 by the Anchor Brewing Company of San Francisco to celebrate its tenth anniversary. Calling upon the advice of archaeologist Solomon Katz of the University of Pennsylvania, they created "Essay, August 1989", a beer designed as a replica of the beer the Ancient Sumerians drank 5000 years ago; the recipe was based on the Hymn to Ninkasi. Apparently the beer was very good but, as it didn't contain hops, had a very short shelf-life.

Another historical beer created at Katz's instigation is, however, still available. This is "Midas Touch", brewed by the Dogfish Head Brewery in Delaware, and is based on molecular analysis of the remains of the funeral banquet accorded to the famous King Midas of Phrygia in the 8th century BC. The basic ingredients are barley, muscat grapes, thyme honey and saffron.

Beer was an important part of ancient Egyptian society too – to the extent that the hieroglyph meaning "food" allied a piece of bread and a jug of beer. Like the Sumerians, the Egyptians made beer from a base of unbaked bread dough (a technique still in use today), adding dates to the mix to improve the flavour.

By 1300BC the Egyptians had produced the first liquor licences, introducing a scheme to regulate beer shops.

Non-alcoholic beer is not as recent an invention as one might think. The Ancient Egyptians came up with it about 1000BC.

The Egyptian god of beer and brewing was Osiris, who was also the god of agriculture. According to Diodorus, "Wherever a climate did not allow the cultivation of the vine, there Osiris taught the people how to brew the beverage which is made of barley [i.e., beer], and which is not much inferior to wine in scent and potency."

The Egyptians also had the beer goddess Tenenit and the cow goddess Hesat; they called milk the "beer of Hesat".

One of the styles of beer developed by the Egyptians was called *boosa* or *wusa*. It is from this word that our own word "booze" comes.

The bread-based *boosa/wusa* had a constituency closer to porridge than to a potable liquid. In *The Beer of the Bible: A Confirmation of Biblical Accuracy* (1868), the anthropologist James Death proposed that the manna God gave to the Israelites was in fact *boosa*. If this was the case, the relevant Biblical passages can be seen as in praise of God for giving the Israelites the gift of beer, which would fit in with many of the world's other mythologies.

The Greeks and Romans, with their vinicultural traditions, did not take easily to beer, although they certainly drank it. Plato commented that "He was a wise man who invented beer" but certain Greek physicians were less complimentary, theorizing that beer-drinking caused leprosy. The general attitude of the Mediterranean cultures was summed up by Tacitus: "To drink, the Teutons have a horrible brew fermented from barley or wheat, a brew that has only a very distant similarity to wine."

Those maligned Teutons had been brewing since at least 800BC, from which period beer amphorae have been found. The ancient Germans brewed for their own enjoyment but also, like so many other ancient peoples, regarded it as a gift from the gods and offered it in their sacrifices.

In Teutonic mythology, the kobold Biersal lived in family cellars and took responsibility for keeping jugs and bottles clean in return for being given a jug of beer daily.

Despite their attitude toward beer, when the Romans arrived in Britain and discovered the peoples there brewing ale from barley, the newcomers made huge improvements to the process. The British beer tradition that persists to this day can be said to owe its origins to this Roman intervention.

One of the best-known tales in the Gospels concerns the wedding feast at Cana, where Jesus is reported to have turned water into wine . . . except that it was almost certainly beer that he turned the water into. The Middle East was at the time rich in grain but grew hardly any grapes, so wine barely existed; most people outside the Roman aristocracy would never even have seen wine, let alone owned or drunk any. The original Aramaic text doesn't particularize the beverage into which the water was turned beyond describing it as "strong [i.e., alcoholic] drink", a term that usually referred to beer because that was just about the only booze around; it's highly improbable the writer would-n't have specified the beverage had it been something so exotic as wine. It was only when the Bible came to be translated out of Aramaic that the term "strong drink" was replaced by the word "wine".

The same considerations apply to the descriptions of events at the Last Supper, which presents a bit of problem for transubstantiationists everywhere!

Jesus was not the only one. According to the *Vita Sanctae Brigidae*, St Bridget, who was active working with lepers in Belgium around the year 500, at one point answered their pleas for beer by blessing the water she'd readied for her bath so that it turned into beer.

The great Finnish saga the Kalevala indicates the relative importance of beer in the scheme of things so far as the ancient Scandinavians were concerned: the creation of the world is covered in about 200 verses whereas over 400 verses are required to describe the creation of beer.

In Finnish mythology the god of fields and corn and barley, Pekko, was unsurprisingly also associated with beer; to him was owed the first-brewed barley beer, sometimes called *pellonpekko*.

According to the Norse Eddas, wine was the perquisite of the gods, beer that of mortals, and mead that of the denizens of the world of the dead.

The Norsemen had a myth to explain the origins of beer. To seal the truce between the Aesir and the Vanir, gods of both factions spat into a bowl and, from the mixture, created Kvasir, the god of knowledge and inspiration, whose primary responsibility was to act as intermediary between the two groups. Unfortunately, the dwarfs murdered him, mixed his blood with honey, and brewed the strong red beer kvas, the Mead of Inspiration; the tale can be seen as an allegory for what happens to knowledge and inspiration when you add alcohol. The dwarfs didn't enjoy their triumph long, because they had to give all their kvas to the giant Suttung in payment of a debt, and he hid it away in three jars in the mountains.

Later Odin, having heard of the brew, decided he wanted a taste. He approached Suttung's sister Gunnlod, whom the giant had charged with guarding the three jars. Odin persuaded her that allowing him just a sip from each jar could surely do no harm, but he took advantage of her kindness and drained all three. He then flew off in the form of an eagle. As he flew, he spilled some of the kvas from the sky, which was how we mortals discovered it. Soon it was found that fermented beetroot juice offered an acceptable substitute in appearance, taste and effect for the original Mead of Inspiration.

The beer of the gods themselves was brewed by Aegir. In his hall the beer tankards had the common folktale property that they never needed to be filled. Aegir used a brew-kettle given to him by Thor, who had taken it from the sea giant Hymir. Hymir will have his revenge for Thor's theft (among much else) at Ragnarok, when he will be commander of the fearful ship Naglfar, made entirely from the nails of the dead.

In Valhalla, too, there was endless ale, although its origins were rather different: it flowed without cease from the udders of a goat called Heidrun.

The Vikings brewed beer not just on land but also aboard their longships, and made extensive resort to it during their marauding campaigns, especially as a means of gearing themselves up to become berserkers. A charming habit they had was using the skulls of their enemies as beer mugs; the Scandinavian toast *Sköl!* comes from the word *scole*, meaning "skull". In place of hops, the Vikings used juniper berries.

One reason the Vikings and their contemporaries drank so much beer was that the fermentation killed harmful bacteria – in other words, beer was a far more reliably safe source of liquid sustenance than water. Because beer was so much safer than water, it became the custom in Europe from around 1200 to use it in preference to water for baptisms.

Known to the Welsh as Govannon, Goibnu was son of the great Irish/Celtic goddess Danu. He made the weaponry for the Tuatha Dé Danann, manufactured swords that always struck true, and did the other things the smiths of the gods usually do. But it was his skill as a brewer that really set him apart: anyone who drank the beer he brewed was granted eternal life.

Lithuanian mythology regarded beer as so important that not just one but a triumvirate of deities was concerned with it: Ragutis was the god of beer, Ragutiene the goddess of beer, and Raugupatis the god of fermentation.

The Zulu people of Southern Africa worshipped Mbaba–Mwana–Waresa, the goddess of the rainbow, agriculture, rain and the harvest; most significantly to the Zulus, she gave humankind the gift of beer.

The Dogon people of Mali had the goddess Yasigi, usually depicted dancing and holding a beer ladle. She was responsible for dancing, masks and beer.

The Mexican beer pulque was created by the Totonac goddess Mayahuel . . . or by the Aztec god Tezcatzontecatl. Also of importance was Ometotchtli, leader of a group of beings called the Centzon–Totochtin, or "Infinite Rabbits". This group repre-

WOMEN AND BREWING

Up until the late Middle Ages, in Western culture brewing was a task left to the women, as before then beer was considered a basic foodstuff rather than a luxury. It was because of its status as a foodstuff that the legal penalties for providing short measure or a poor beer were so draconian; bad alewives could look forward to a flogging at the very least.

The tradition of women and beer goes back a very long way, and is found all over the world; we recall that the Babylonian beer deity Ninkasi was a goddess rather than a god. The anthropologist Alan Eames has commented in an interview with Robert Lauriston: "In the Amazonian Indian myths relating to the production of their manioc and corn beers, it's always a woman who was first tricked or seduced into making the first beer. . . . In archaeological sites in Egypt and the Sudan, in 5000-year-old Sumerian cuneiform manuscripts, among contemporary tribal people and rural farmers from Peru to Norway, you find the exact same thing: women making beer, same way, same basket, same pot, same rituals. Tibetan beers are very similar to Amazonian manioc beers. The nomads of the Yellow River area of Mongolia have these little portable breweries that go on horseback, and the women take them wherever they go. . . . In my opinion, women have maintained power and status in macho, male-dominated hunter–gatherer societies by developing their skills as brewsters. . . . [S]ince beer was a critical dietary staple, women just took control of it."

In Medieval Europe, women were generally responsible for brewing in the home and also for brewing the ale to be consumed in public taverns. Even so, alewives could hold the licence for their tavern only if widowed; otherwise it had to remain in the husband's name.

"Give me a woman who truly loves beer and I will conquer the world."
Kaiser Wilhelm II

sented the infinite ways in which human beings can be affected
by intoxication.

The Cuna Indians of Panama worship a cultural hero called
Ibeorgun, who taught their ancestors the fundamentals of life –
what to eat, how to cook, how to celebrate girls' attainment of
puberty, and much else – not least being the art of brewing their
maize beer.

The Jivaro Indians of Ecuador are best known for their refusal
to treat with the outside world and for their practice of head-
hunting and shrinking the heads of their victims – there was a
fair international trade in the shrunken heads during the first
half of the 20th century – but the Jivaro are also of note for their
consumption of manioc beer: the men each consume per day an
astonishing 3–4 gallons of this potent brew, the women a "mere"
1–2 gallons, and children just half a gallon. The brewing is done
entirely by the women; an important part of the process is that
the women chew handfuls of manioc root and spit it into the
mash.

It wasn't only women who brewed beer in Dark Age and
Medieval Europe: monks did it too. Primarily this was for
reasons of monastic self-sufficiency (some convents also started
breweries), although obviously of course monks were men who
had withdrawn themselves from society's main male pool and
could thus be seen as legitimately taking on women's duties.
Certainly they made significant contributions to the develop-
ment of beer, and to this day some of the finest beers are of
monastic origin. The status of the tradition that the 12th-
century St Hildegard of Bingen was the person who introduced
the use of hops to brewing is uncertain.

"History flows forward on rivers of beer."
Anonymous

The hops of Bohemia were so prized in the 10th century that Wenceslas (*c*907–929), Prince-Duke of Bohemia – the Good King Wenceslas of the carol – issued an edict prescribing the death penalty for anyone exporting cuttings from which new plants could be grown.

The Patron Saint of Brewers is recognized by the Roman Catholic Church as Saint Arnold. He was born in Austria, entered the priesthood, and by 612 was Bishop of Metz. At the time, there was little understanding of the nature of disease, and not everyone realized insanitary drinking water was a major cause of illness. Bishop Arnold did, and repeatedly hammered it home to his congregations that they should drink beer rather than water for their own safety.

In 627 he retreated to a monastery near Remiremont, in France, and there he died in 640. The following year, the citizens of Metz asked that their beloved bishop be reburied in their city. As the procession from Remiremont passed through the town of Champignuelles, the bearers took a break. Imagine their distress when they discovered the local tavern had almost run out of beer: there was enough left for only one mugful, which they would have to share.

The miracle that brought Arnold his sainthood – and eventually his patron sainthood – was that this single tankard of beer never ran dry . . .

The idea of taxing beer owes its origins, at least in the West, to Christian belief and the Roman Catholic Church. Until Louis Pasteur's work in the 1870s (see page 25) no one had much of a clue as to how brewing actually worked: it just did. Or, rather, God intervened to make it happen. The trouble with this explanation was that some batches turned out bad; since obviously God couldn't be the one to blame, the Devil must have interfered in some way. It became the practice in the Middle Ages, in order to stop the Devil's meddling, to put icons or other

THE REINHEITSGEBOT

In the 1490s there appeared in Augsburg, Bavaria, the Western world's first food regulation, and its subject was beer. In 1516 Duke Wilhelm IV formalized the regulation and applied it to the whole of Bavaria. This was the famous Reinheitsgebot ("Purity Regulation"), whose (translated) text reads:

- We hereby proclaim and decree, by Authority of our Province, that henceforth in the Duchy of Bavaria, in the country as well as in the cities and marketplaces, the following rules apply to the sale of beer:
- From Michaelmas to Georgi, the price for one maß [about a litre] or one kopf [container holding just less than one maß] is not to exceed one pfennig Munich value, and from Georgi to Michaelmas the maß shall not be sold for more than two pfennigs of the same value, the kopf not more than three hellers [half pfennig].
- If this not be adhered to, the punishment stated below shall be administered.
- Should any person brew, or otherwise have, other beer than March beer, it is not to be sold at any higher than one pfennig per maß.
- Furthermore, we wish to emphasize that in future in all cities, markets and in the country, the only ingredients used for the brewing of beer must be barley, hops and water. Whosoever knowingly disregards or transgresses upon this ordinance shall be punished by the Court

authorities' confiscating such barrels of beer, without fail.

•••• Should, however, an innkeeper in the country, city or markets buy two or three pails of beer [containing 60 maß] and sell it again to the common peasantry, he alone shall be permitted to charge one heller more for the maß or the kopf than mentioned above. Furthermore, should there arise a scarcity and subsequent price increase of the barley (also considering that the times of harvest differ, due to location), We, the Bavarian Duchy, shall have the right to order curtailments for the good of all concerned.

The order specified that the only ingredients permitted in the making of beer were barley, water and hops – no yeast. At the time, it wasn't known that yeast played any part in fermentation; that was to wait until the 1870s when Louis Pasteur published the results of his investigation of the subject (see page 25).

The restriction to barley of the grain used in brewing was in order to end the competition between brewers and bakers for the grains wheat and rye – and the consequent price hikes. In other words, this particular specification was less an aesthetic measure than an effort to keep the price of bread down.

The Reinheitsgebot was applied to Germany as a whole in 1871 and survived until 1987, when it was repealed by the EC as part of the breaking down of trade barriers – before that, many perfectly good beers from elsewhere in Europe were prohibited in Germany. Some German brewers in fact still adhere to the Reinheitsgebot – or at least claim to.

Christian symbols prominently around the brewhouse. Better still was to have the local priest bless each batch during the brewing process; this was known as the Rite of Signage, and the priest was typically paid four pints of beer for it. When some priests became greedy and demanded more, laws had to be enacted to regulate payment. Soon after, it occurred to the Church that the priest could perhaps better be spending his time elsewhere: so long as the brewer paid the fee to the Church, the blessing could be done at a distance, in a general sort of a way. The coming of the French Revolution in 1789 was the beginning of the end for this particular form of taxation, but the Church's loss was seen as a chance for the government's gain . . .

When Columbus made his famous voyage to the New World in 1492 he discovered that the indigenous people there were well acquainted with beer and the art of brewing. The beer they made was derived from corn and the sap of the black birch.

During the reign of King Henry VIII of England, the ladies at his court were granted a daily ration of a gallon of ale – that's about 4.5 litres or 9.6 US pints. His daughter, Elizabeth I, was another sturdy toper, and the gossip at court was that she could drink any man under the table. She preferred strong beer, and her favourite breakfast was bread and ale.

In 1632 the youthful patients at the Norwich Children's Hospital in the UK were each rationed two gallons of beer *per diem*: beer was regarded as a food rather than as an alcoholic treat. One assumes the drink in question was small beer; even so, the youngsters must have . . . well, slept soundly, at least. Beer's restorative influence – or perhaps merely as always the danger of the water supply – was recognized also at St Bartholomew's Hospital in London where, between 1687 and the suspension of the policy by the abstinence-conscious

Victorians in 1860, the patients' diet included three pints of beer a day; the hospital supplied the need with its own brewery. In between beers, the patients might be administered, for strictly medicinal purposes, doses of either possett (warm milk curdled with ale) or caudle (gruel, spices and ale or wine).

On October 17, 1814, in St Giles, London, a brewery tank containing 3500 barrels of beer ruptured, flooding the streets around. Nine people lost their lives and two houses collapsed in what is probably history's greatest "beer disaster".

In 1876 Louis Pasteur published his groundbreaking *Études sur la bière*, in which he announced his revolutionary new flash-heating technique of killing the bacteria in beer so that it could be stored for longer. It was only later that folk realized the same principle could be applied to other things, like milk . . .

The first time beer is known to have been brewed by the European immigrants to the Americas was in 1587, at Sir Walter Ralegh's colony in Virginia. We know this because the colonists requested that better beer be sent from home than the stuff they were making themselves.

When the Pilgrim Fathers made land at Plymouth Rock in 1620 they did so, according to the diary of one of them, because the *Mayflower*'s crew were concerned there might not be enough beer aboard for the journey home unless they got rid of their passengers pretty soon.

The first commercial brewery in the New World, Block & Christiansens, opened in 1612 in the city that was then called New Amsterdam, now New York. It was staffed by professional brewers who'd responded to advertisements placed in the London newspapers by the colonists. Two years later the brewery saw the birth of the first non-native to be born in the New World, Jean Vigne. Perhaps not surprisingly, he grew up to become a brewer himself.

The first brand-named beer in the colonies was brewed around 1632 in New Amsterdam by the Red Lion Brewery.

By 1674 Harvard University had opened its own brewhouse, with students receiving beer with their meals three times a day. Five beer halls in succession were burned down by rioting Divinity students.

One of the first acts of the Continental Congress in 1775 was to make an allowance of a quart of beer per day for soldiers serving in the Revolutionary Army.

One of the most celebrated beer recipes of all time is the one for Small Beer prepared by George Washington in 1754: "Take a large Siffer full of Bran Hops to your taste – Boil these 3 hours[,] strain out 30 Gallns into a cooler[,] put in 3 Gallns molasses while the beer is scalding hot or rather draw the molasses into the cooler & strain the beer on it while boiling hot. Let this stand till it is little more than Blood warm[,] then put in a quart of yeast[. I]f the weather is very cold cover it over with a blanket & let it work in the Cooler 24 hours[,] then put it into the Cask – leave [. . .] the Bung open till it is almost done Working – Bottle it that day [one] Week [after] it was brewed."

The first proposal to tax beer in the New World came in 1789 from James Madison, who asked Congress to impose a duty of

THE DANGERS OF OVERTAXATION

Governments all over the world have delighted
in taxing beer, especially since about the
middle of the 20th century.
They should take note of history.
In 1888 in Munich the local citizenry,
offended by vicious hikes in the price of their
beer, mounted a full-scale riot that became
known as the Battle of Salvator.

eight cents per barrel not as a means to raise money *per se* but
as a way of promoting the "manufacture of beer in every State
in the Union".

In 1809 Madison, by now President, wanted to create a cabinet
appointment of Secretary of Beer.

The first known lager brewed in the US was made in 1840 in
Philadelphia by John Wagner, who had bought the nation's first
lager yeast from a Bavarian brewery.

The big surge in US beer-drinking came in the second half of
the 19th century, and owes its origins on the one hand to the
Industrial Revolution and on the other to new waves of immigrants from Germany, who brought their expertise in lager-
brewing with them; among the famous names involved were
Anheuser, Busch, Coors, Pabst, Miller, Schlitz and Stroh. By
1880 there were reckoned to be some 2300 breweries in the US,
although this number dropped off after a while owing to
commercial competition and mergers.

A BRIEF HISTORY OF PROHIBITION

*"Prohibition makes you want to cry into your beer
and denies you the beer to cry into."*
– Don Marquis

IN MEMORIAM
JOHN BARLEYCORN
BORN B.C.
DIED JAN.16,1920
RESURRECTION ?

The abstinence movement came to the USA in 1836 with the formation of the United States Temperance Union. By 1915 the Anti-Saloon League persuaded Congress to vote on a constitutional amendment prohibiting liquor, but this failed to meet the two-thirds majority required (although it did obtain a simple majority vote, of 197 to 190). However, when in January 1919 the matter was put to the vote again, the abstainers triumphed as Congress ratified the 18th Amendment, prohibiting the manufacture, import or sale of "intoxicating liquors". In October of that year the meaning of "intoxicating liquor" was defined by the Volstead Act as anything with over 0.5% alcohol. (No one seems to have worried about babies' gripe water, which habitually has a higher alcohol content than this.)

When Prohibition came into full force in 1920, beer and cider drinkers were the hardest hit: bootleggers focused on the far more convenient hard liquors. The existing breweries tried to take up the slack – and stay in business – by producing "near beers", drinks that supposedly tasted like beer but met the stringent limitations on alcohol content. The demand for these was not high (even when people thought to lace near beer with neat alcohol): of the 1400 or so US breweries in existence before Prohibition, only about 160 would survive it. By 1926 the Wet Party had been formed with the sole purpose of ending Prohibition, but popular attention turned to more pressing matters in 1929 with the onset of the Great Depression. Even so, 1930 saw the few surviving breweries get together to form the American Brewers' Association.

Some of the brewers became remarkably resourceful in their efforts to survive the drought. Anheuser–Busch became particularly versatile: the company produced not just obvious spinoffs like bakery yeast and barley malt syrup but also ice cream, and it diversified into the manufacture of refrigerators and truck bodies.

In 1932 the Democrats and their Presidential candidate, Franklin Roosevelt, made the repeal of Prohibition part of their platform. Whether for this reason or because of his plans to cope with the Depression, Roosevelt took the White House with overwhelming popular support, and on December 5, 1933, the 21st Amendment was passed to end Prohibition.

"I think this would be a good time for a beer."
– Franklin D. Roosevelt
(upon signing the New Deal, paving the way
for the repeal of Prohibition)

*"Instead of giving money to found colleges to promote learning,
why don't they pass a constitutional amendment
prohibiting anybody from learning anything? If it works as good
as the Prohibition one did, why, in five years we would
have the smartest race of people on earth."*
– Will Rogers

The railroads and refrigeration were the two technological developments that really made beer the US national drink. The first national brand was Budweiser, brewed by Anheuser–Busch and distributed via a network of regionally based ice houses by means of refrigerated railway cars.

Before about 1890, the primary source of potable alcohol in the US was distilled spirits, but in that year beer took over the lead. Within a few years, Pabst recorded a milestone by becoming the first brewer to sell over a million barrels in a year.

When Theodore Roosevelt set off for an African safari in 1909, he took over 500 gallons of beer with him.

"Great indeed the reputation of the ancient beer –
Said to make the feeble hardy,
Famed to dry the tears of women,
Famed to cheer the broken-hearted,
Make the timid brave and mighty,
Fill the heart with joy and gladness,
Fill the mind with wisdom,
Fill the tongue with ancient legends,
Only makes the fool more foolish."
The Kalevala

*"**Abstainer:** A weak person who yields to the*
temptation of denying himself a pleasure."
Ambrose Bierce, *The Devil's Dictionary*

"Life isn't all beer and skittles, but beer and skittles,
or something better of the same sort, must form a good part
of every Englishman's education."
Thomas Hughes, *Tom Brown's Schooldays*

THE BREWS
REVIVAL

As in the early years of the 20th century, commercial competition brutally whittled down the number of US breweries after the initial surge that followed the end of Prohibition. By 1984, out of a post-Prohibition peak of 756, there were only 83 breweries left, and the situation was actually worse than that, because those 83 breweries were owned by a mere 44 brewers. In reality, the only important players were a small number of massive brewing companies, and US beer drinkers unwilling to resort to beers imported from Europe, Mexico and Japan were offered an astonishingly limited choice of beers that for the most part tasted (a) much the same and (b) not very good – indeed, domestic US beers had become the laughing-stock of the world.

A decade or two earlier, the UK had suffered a similar malaise, thanks to the tied-house system, whereby (to simplify) pubs were run by breweries and therefore stocked only that brewery's beers plus, sometimes, one or two supposedly specialty brews like Guinness. The beer scene was one of large brewery companies becoming ever larger as they swallowed smaller, more traditional ones, often keeping the name but "modernizing" systems so that once-fine ales became identikit fizzy keg-conditioned pasteurized beers of uniform blandness. The rot was stopped thanks to a public movement that began in 1971 with the formation in England – by Michael Hardman, Graham Lees, Jim Makin and Bill Mellor – of the Campaign for Real Ale (CAMRA). The aim of CAMRA was to protect and revive the fortunes of traditional cask-conditioned ale, and the organization mounted campaigns in the media as well as enacting mock funerals every time a cask-conditioning brewery was closed down. CAMRA's cause was assisted by the boom in home brewing, whereby people discovered they could make significantly better (and significantly cheaper) beer at home than they could buy in the pub. The movement grew, and smaller breweries opened up or were revived in droves; in parallel, the larger brewers realized they had to change their ways or go under.

CAMRA has been an astonishing success, and today it is a rare pub in the UK that does not offer a selection of draught real ales, while even supermarkets stock a wide range of fine and imported beers in cans and bottles.

CAMRA now has over 150 "chapters" in the UK as well as overseas branches in Argentina, Australia, Belgium, Canada, Denmark, Kenya, South Africa and Switzerland, not to mention the US, where there are branches for Florida/Southeast USA, Massachusetts & New England, North Carolina & Northeast USA, and Nebraska & Midwest USA.

CAMRA was one of the three founder organizations of the European Beer Consumers' Union (EBCU), formed in Bruges in May 1990; the other two organizations were PINT (Netherlands) and Objectieve Bierproevers (Belgium). (Objectieve Bierproevers was replaced in 2002 by the Belgian association Zythios.) Similar organizations have since joined from Austria, Denmark, Finland, France, Italy, Norway, Poland, Sweden and Switzerland. The stated aims and objectives of the ECBU are:

- ◆ preservation of European beer culture
- ◆ support of traditional breweries
- ◆ representation of beer drinkers

The parallel revival in the fortunes of US beer, although its full flowering came later than its counterpart in Europe, in fact began slightly earlier. Its origin can be traced to the purchase in 1965 by washing-machine heir Fritz Maytag of San Francisco's Anchor Brewing Company. Founded in 1896, this brewer had an honourable tradition but, in attempting to adapt to the bland-beer market of the 1960s, it was fast declining. Maytag promptly reintroduced traditional techniques and recipes and turned Anchor into a hugely successful company – the first craft brewery in the US since pre-Prohibition times. Its product Anchor Steam is today regarded as a rare example of an indigenous US beer style.

One of the things that hindered the beer revival in the US was a set of well intentioned laws that had been introduced after Prohibition. Seeking to retain diversity and avoid the perils of the tied-house system, Congress had determined that there should be a three-tier structure of the beer industry: brewer, distributor and retailer of any beer must be independently owned. However, this made it very difficult for a craft brewery to get into business, and the legal tangles facing anyone who wanted to open a brewpub were formidable. These laws have been progressively relaxed to allow the beer revolution to continue apace.

In 1977 the New Albion Brewing Company of Sonoma, California, was the first to open in the US of what are now called microbreweries; it lasted for only five years, but it represented the shape of things to come so far as US beer was concerned. Its pioneering move was followed in 1979 by the DeBakker Brewing Company in California, in 1980 by the Boulder Brewery (later renamed Rockies Brewing) in Colorado and Cartwright Brewing in Oregon, and in 1981 by the Sierra Nevada Brewing Company in California. Of these, only Boulder/Rockies and Sierra Nevada still survive, but this high failure rate has not been a pattern: in 1995, for example, 308 new breweries opened in the US while only 32 closed. Precise figures are hard to obtain, but all told there are now about 1400 microbreweries and about 800 brewpubs operating in the US.

By the dawn of the 21st century, the USA, whose beers just a couple of decades earlier had justifiably been the butt of countless jokes worldwide, was regarded – despite continuing marketplace dominance by the big few brewers – as the country producing probably the finest range of beers in the world. Important in this context was the formation in 2000 of the US-based international organization RateBeer. From its own mission statement: "RateBeer was founded in May 2000 by Bill Buchanan as a forum for beer lovers to come together and share their opinions of beer and breweries. Established and maintained by dedicated volunteers, RateBeer has become the premier resource for consumer-driven beer ratings, features on beer culture and industry events, weekly beer-related editorials, and an internationally recognized, semi-annual RateBeer Best competition. The community now has thousands of members from more than 60 countries who have rated tens of thousands of beers from around the world. Our mission is to provide independent, unbiased, consumer-driven information about beer and breweries and to enhance the image and worldwide appreciation of beer."

"Many a man takes to beer, not from the love of beer,
but from a natural craving for the light, warmth, company,
and comfort which is thrown in along with the beer,
and which he cannot get except by buying beer.
Reformers will never get rid of the drink shop
until they can outbid it in the subsidiary attractions which
it offers to its customers."
William Booth

ALL SORTS AND CONDITIONS OF BEER

The world of beer is filled with a profusion of names – not just the brand-names, which are of course legion, but the names of different *styles*. Opening any text concerning beer is too often to be confronted by an intimidating terminological maze. Here is an exercise in untangling.

There are only two basic styles of beers: ales and lagers. These correspond to the two different types of yeast that can be used in beer-brewing.

Ales are top-fermented beers; the yeasts do their stuff at the top of the container, exposed to the air, and at warmer temperatures (14–38°C/58–100°F), and thus generally work faster than their bottom-fermenting cousins. Ales can be brewed from maize, manioc, rice, fruit, sorghum, millet, grasses and just about any other grain you might imagine. Although we generally think of ales and hops in the same breath, in fact the vast majority of ales brewed through history have eschewed the use of hops.

Lagers are bottom-fermented brews: the yeasts do their stuff at the bottom of the container, away from the air, and at cooler temperatures (4–10°C/35–50°F), and thus generally work more slowly than their top-fermenting cousins. The lower temperature means the brew is protected from souring micro-organisms, so fewer hops are required and the beer need not be raised to the same alcoholic strength in order to "keep". (This is not to say that lagers are necessarily weaker than ales. Some of the strongest beers available are lagers.) The longer period of fermentation makes for a more mellow – or, as ale partisans might describe it, blander – flavour.

Ale was the prevalent beer style up until the latter part of the 19th century, when advances in technology – thermometry, refrigeration and bottling – gave lager dominance. The big turning point came in 1842 with the invention at Plzen in Bohemia (now in the Czech Republic) of **Pilsner** (a.k.a. Pils, Pilsener, Pilzen, Plzensky). This lager was attractively pale, had a good but not aggressive flavour, and was of moderate strength. It became a worldwide craze in the 1850s, the first Pilsner reaching the New World in 1856. Although fashions are now drifting back slowly in favour of ales, lager is still by a long way the world's dominant brew, with only Belgium and the UK being strong redoubts of ale preference.

Lagers are typically best drunk chilled; ales are typically best drunk at room temperature. This is, whatever partisans on either side might say, one of the very few demarcations between the two styles affecting the consumer: there is so much overlap in characteristics of beers produced in either style that, over much of the range of beers, it takes an educated palate to determine with certainty whether a particular brew is an ale or a lager. There are dark, fruity, potent lagers and pale, subtle, fresh-tasting, low-strength ales. Further to confuse the picture, there are also hybrids, where (say) ale yeasts are used in a lager-style fermentation process.

"A little bit of beer is divine medicine."
Paracelsus

"A meal of bread, cheese and beer constitutes the chemically perfect food."
Queen Elizabeth I

ALE TYPES

Here are some of the types of ales you're likely to encounter:

Bitter

Known in Scotland as **Heavy**. These beers need not in fact be bitter at all; the style got its name when English brewers first began using hops in the early 16th century. Most draught ales served in the UK are bitters, although lagers have made significant incursions in recent decades. Conversely, whereas a couple of decades ago it was unheard-of to find a draught bitter in a US bar, they're now a quite common presence.

Brown Ale

There are three distinctive styles of brown ales – two in the UK and a third in the US. The brown ale of the southern part of England – often called **Mild** – is typically a fruity, filling beer, usually of fairly low alcohol content. The browns more typical of the northern part of Britain are a different beast, as typified by the famous **Newcastle Brown**. What is called **American Brown Ale** is different again, having less of the caramel/butterscotch taste of the UK browns and being somewhat hoppier.

Pale Ale

In the UK these are essentially the equivalents of bitters but in bottles or, more recently, cans. Of particular note is **IPA**, or **India Pale Ale** (sometimes called **Export Pale Ale**). This came into existence when the British colonials in India requested that their favourite brews be sent out from home. The long ocean voyage, however, tended to destroy the beers. Eventually a brewer named Hodgson created a stronger, hoppier beer specifically for the colonies, in the (correct) belief that the increased alcohol and acidic content would protect the brew. An added bonus, it was discovered, was that, during the long period of gentle motion at sea, the beer picked up some nice woody flavours from the casks.

American pale ales – often called **Amber Ales** – were made in imitation of their UK equivalents. The style almost died out during the 19th century and the first half of the 20th; by 1960 there was only one left, **Ballantine Pale Ale**. Since then there has been a revival.

Belgian pale ales likewise originated in imitation of UK styles but much later, around the middle of the 20th century. They taste rather different from the originals because the Belgians use different yeast strains.

Porter

A style introduced in 1722 by London brewer Ralph Harwood. In the Shoreditch region where he operated his pub and brewery, it became the fashion among market porters to prefer a mix called Three Threads: one third bitter, one third aged brown ale, and one third fresh (still fermenting) brown ale. It was tedious for the publican to have all three on tap, so Harwood devised an ale, which he called **Entire**, that he claimed matched Three Threads: high in hops, it was allowed to mature for several months. His customers agreed and the ale became popular, but called Porter because of its first aficionados.

Stout

Porter spread to Ireland, but was slow to catch on there. In 1778 the Irish brewer Arthur Guinness began to create a strong version of it, which he called Stout Porter. Within a few decades the Guinness Brewery was preparing nothing else and had become the largest brewery in the world, with Stout (as it was by now called) established as the Irish national drink.

The style is today brewed in many parts of the world and in a number of different styles. **Sweet Stout**, often known as **Milk Stout**, is typified by Mackeson, an English beer; the sugar used in brewing Sweet Stout is lactose, hence the alternative name. **Double Stout** is a term referring to stouts modelled on Guinness Foreign Extra Stout, a stronger version of the Irish original. In a rather different category is our next style.

Imperial Stout

This was created by the London Brewer Barclay & Perkins in the late 18th century for shipment to the Baltic; it was a great favourite of Catherine the Great. It was more of a barley wine (see below) than a mainstream ale. The onset of the Russian Revolution destroyed this export market; today Barclay & Perkins (now owned by Courage) make just one annual batch for connoisseurs. The name has, however, survived in association with other, similar strong dark ales.

In the early 1980s brewers in the US began preparing an imitation Imperial Stout, often calling it *Russian Imperial Stout* in recognition of its origins.

Barley Wine

Essentially these are just very strong ales, their alcohol content (8–15%) pushing well up into the wine-strength range. They require an extra long time to age – anywhere from six months to several years – and often wine yeasts are utilized because better able to handle the alcohol levels in the brew.

In the US these beers must be called *Barleywine-Style Ales* because of laws prohibiting the sale of beer–wine mixtures or any drink that might purport to be such a mixture.

Wheat Beer

Known also as *Weissbiers*, these employ wheat/wheat malt to replace some of the barley/barley malt used in their conventionally brewed counterparts, and are popular in parts of Mainland Europe – especially Belgium, Germany and, increasingly, North America. This is not a new style; indeed, a principal reason for the introduction of the Reinheitsgebot (see page 22) was to shift the base grain of beer from wheat to barley so as to protect wheat supplies for bakers from the depredations of brewers. Wheat beers are top-fermented, which means they are definitely ales, but they are aged at very cold temperatures, thereby having some affinity with lagers.

Golden Ale

A US style, sometimes called *Blond Ale*, developed as an equivalent to the UK's Pale Ale, but considerably paler in colour (and often confused by drinkers with lagers) because the malts are paler.

Belgian Beers

These are sufficiently diverse and distinctive that they are often regarded as in a separate family distinct from ales and lagers. The subvarieties are:

- *Belgian Ale* Generally golden to deep amber, and flavourful.
- *Lambic* Wheat beers brewed without the addition of yeast – i.e., using the wild yeasts present in the atmosphere.
- *Faro* A Lambic brewed with extra sugar for sweetness.
- *Gueuse* A sour beer made by blending old and new Lambics.
- *Belgian/Flanders Brown Ale* A brown ale that lacks hoppy taste but compensates with its own spiciness.
- *Belgian/Flanders Red Ale* Of varying redness, lacks hoppy taste, but has a pleasant sour/vinegary component to the taste.
- *Belgian Strong Ale* Stronger than normal ale, very malty but also very hoppy.
- *Saison* Copper-coloured beer rather like less potent Belgian Strong Ale, with an added spiciness.
- *Witbier* A wheat beer with a mild flavour.

*"Do not cease to drink beer, to eat, to intoxicate thyself,
to make love, and to celebrate the good days."*
Egyptian Proverb

LAGER TYPES

*Here are some of the types of lagers you're
likely to encounter:*

Pilsner

Originally from what is now the Czech Republic, the archetype
of lager beers, and the style that American Pale Lagers (see
below) and many others seek to emulate.

Bock

Originally a Bavarian beer that was brewed in the late autumn,
aged over the winter, and drunk for the six weeks following the
first day of spring. This relatively strong beer is traditionally
dark, but today there are also many pale varieties.

Märzenbier

By tradition this was the last beer made during the winter brewing season; it was then aged until the Oktoberfest – hence the
alternative name of ***Oktoberfest Beer***.

Vienna Beer

The original Oktoberfest Beer was in fact a Vienna Beer. This
style was developed in the early 1840s by the Viennese brewer
Anton Dreher, and is an amber lager of moderately light taste
and strength.

German Dark Lagers

Although Pilsner is often described as the first lager, in fact the
earliest commercial lagers were produced at the Spaten
Brewery, and they were dark, brewed in a style that had been
used in Bavaria for some centuries. Beers in this ***Dunkel*** style
are still made by a couple of the larger brewers and countless
small ones.

German Pale Lagers

There are a host of these, of which perhaps the internationally best-known is ***Kölsch***, which is a specialty of the Cologne region; it has a fruity, sometimes slightly sourish taste.

Rauchbier

The term means "smoked beer", and refers to the fact that the malt used to produce the beer is smoked over wood fires, imparting a smoky flavour to the beer. This was the traditional way of heating the malt; when new ways were found, Rauchbier fell from popular grace precisely because its smoky taste was regarded as a demerit. Luckily a few brewers persisted in the old way, and the smoky flavour is now highly esteemed.

American Pale Lagers

All these were originally modelled on Pilsner, but as time went on and breweries conglomerated, they degenerated to become the American generic beer. Since the onset of the American beer revolution, a few good examples of American Pale Lagers have emerged, but generally speaking the style is not much admired.

There are also a few ***American Dark Lagers*** of note; at their best these taste not unlike stout.

HYBRID TYPES

*Here are some of the types of hybrid beers you're
likely to encounter:*

Altbier

Almost all German beers are now lagers, but there are exceptions. One is ***Dortmunder***, an ale today brewed almost exclusively for export. The Altbiers are, strictly speaking, also ales, in that they are top-fermented; thereafter, however, they are given a lager-style cold-aging treatment. ("*Alt*" means "old", referring to the old – i.e., top-fermenting – mode of fermentation, which was largely replaced by lager-style bottom fermentation.) Altbiers tend to have a fairly strong hoppy and malty taste.

Cream Ale

A style that originated in US efforts to produce a light-bodied ale. Cream Ales are top-fermented in the ale style but given the long, cold processing of lagers – from which they're rather difficult to distinguish except for their aromatic taste.

Steam Beer

Also known as ***California Common Beer***, this was first developed during the Gold Rush, around the end of the 19th century. Although lager yeasts are used, the beer is fermented in the ale style; this is because it was difficult to achieve the cold temperatures for lager fermentation in the Californian climate.

ASSORTED BREWS

There are of course dozens of substyles of each of the main styles.
Probably no list could be complete, but here are a few:

Abbaye

Not so much a style as an appellation, referring to those beers produced by Trappist monasteries; there are only six such breweries in the world, and their products are very highly regarded indeed. The breweries are ***Chimay***, ***La Trappe*** (***Koningshoeven***), ***Orval***, ***Rochefort***, ***Westmalle*** and ***Westvleteren***.

Abbey

Any beer produced by a commercial brewer under a licence granted by a monastic order.

Algarroba Beer

The traditional beer made by the Chaco Indians of Latin
America. It's a bean-based ale.

Amazon Black Beer

Traditionally brewed by the Amazonian Indians using manioc
and, in place of hops, lupine. The Europeans who discovered
these beers replicated them as best they could in black lagers.
The only one you're likely ever to come across outside Brazil is
Xingu Black Beer.

Apache Corn

Brewed traditionally by the Apaches, this was a corn-based beer
"improved" by the addition of poisonous plants like jimson that
have hallucinogenic properties in low concentrations. In the
1880s such beers were banned in the US, but localized variants
can still be found in some parts of South America.

Berliner Weisse

A beer named for its colour, which is white. Strictly speaking,
Berliner Weisse must be brewed only in Berlin, but the style is
(rarely) found in other parts of the world. This author found an
excellent white beer in Canada.

Bière de Garde/Bière de Paris

Bières de Garde, from northwestern France, are strong beers,
either lagers or ales, that are brewed in winter and conditioned
in the bottle so as to last through the summer months. *Bières de
Paris* are the Parisian equivalent, but exclusively lagers.

Birch Beer

An unmalted brew made in North America from honey, birch

twigs and birch sap. It was slow-fermenting and potent. Today the term "birch beer" refers to an unfermented equivalent – i.e., birch beer (like ginger beer) has become exclusively a soft drink.

Burton Ale
The original Pale Ale, as brewed at Burton-on-Trent, England.

Chicha
A sacred brew, a corn-based beer brewed by the indigenous peoples of Latin America and parts of what is now the south-western US. There are many varieties, ranging from the nonalcoholic **Chicha Morada** – the original Near Beer! – to **Chicha de Jora**, which is of spiritous strength.

Chili Beer
Originally made in South and Central America, this is beer made with the addition of chili peppers; today it is also made by a few enterprising US microbreweries. Often bottled with a whole chili pepper included so you can see what you're getting into.

Chocolate Beer
Beer brewed with the addition of unsweetened bakers' chocolate. Until recently this was primarily in the province of home brewers, but it has slowly been gaining in commercial popularity.

Eisbock
Beer whose alcohol level has been increased by freezing the liquid, then removing the water-ice. This practice is banned in the US under the same regulations forbidding the making of applejack (though see Ice Beer, below), but in fact Eisbocks are

nowhere near the potency of applejacks, usually weighing in at about 10% alcohol. The style has adherents in Germany, where it is made by a few recognized brewers.

Festbier

German beers done in various styles – usually the Märzenbier style – for the various winter solstitial holidays.

Fruit Beer

Any beer in which fruit has been included in the fermentation and has given detectable flavour to the finished brew. These are not to be confused with recent commercially marketed items comprising Malt Liquors to which fruit flavours have been added.

Ginger Beer

Nowadays thought of almost exclusively as a soft drink, ginger beer was historically a beer brewed with ginger used in place of hops to counter the sweetness of the malt. Some Spiced Beers use ginger as a flavouring.

Grand Cru

Term used of Belgian ales to indicate that they're "special vintage" – i.e., given a long aging period and usually strong. There's no particular regulation of the term, however, so often it's used merely as a marketing ploy.

Heather Ale

The first beer brewed in Britain – in Scotland, by the Picts, who kept the precise recipe a secret. The heather apparently performed the same function as hops later would, but supposedly also gave the ale hallucinogenic properties. As it was also fearsomely strong, the Romans – and just about everyone else – attributed their difficulty in suppressing the Picts, or even taming them, to the influence of Heather Ale. The secret of the brew supposedly died in the 4th century with the death in battle of the Pictish King Trost of the Long Knife. Heather-based ales have been brewed in more recent times, but lack the wondrous properties of the lost original . . . if indeed those properties existed outside legend.

Herbal Beer
Beer made using herbal substances as an ingredient in the brewing process. Many of these – such as birch beer, ginger beer and root beer – are now known almost exclusively as soft drinks. Ginseng is growing in popularity as a herbal additive.

Ice Beer
The name used in North America for various equivalents of Eisbock (q.v.). There is a loophole in the US law that bans the distillation of drinks using freezing, which is that it specifies the liquid volume of the brew must not be less at the end of the process than at the beginning. Certain brewing techniques begin with a reduced amount of water, the "missing" water being added later. This nicety permits the use of the Eisbock method during manufacture.

Irish Ale
A style of ale that originated in Ireland but is now more often found in the US; essentially, a pale ale done with caramel malt to give it a reddish colour.

London Ale
As opposed to Burton Ale (q.v.), pale ale brewed in London. The harder waters of the London region gave the beers there

a character distinct from those brewed using the softer waters of northern England.

Malt Liquor

Strong American Pale Lager, brewed primarily for strength without concern about flavour; indeed, special techniques may be used to convert some of the flavour-enhancing elements of the brew to sugars, to add to the amount of fermentable substances present, and thus the final alcohol level. The term "malt liquor" was introduced because certain of the states do not permit beers over a certain strength to be marketed as beers.

Masato

One of the two main types of traditional South American beers, the other being the corn-based Chicha (q.v.). Masato is, by contrast, manioc-based.

Near Beer

Beer with extremely low alcohol content (typically under 0.7%), the alcohol having been removed by distillation. As Luke McLuke sagely remarked, "The man who called it 'near beer' was a bad judge of distance." Such beers were much brewed during Prohibition by brewers desperate to find a way of staying in business. They regained a certain measure of popularity among health- and driving-safety-conscious drinkers later in the 20th century, although few are palatable. A possible exception is *Kaliber*, prepared by Guinness.

Oatmeal Stout

From England, stout brewed with oatmeal (rolled oats or oatflakes) present in the mash, purportedly to increase the nutritional value of the final product. The beer is very dark, and has a full round flavour. Not too much oatmeal can be used, as oats may cause problems during the brewing process.

Oyster Stout

Stout with oysters is a traditional combination, and various brewers have consequently used oyster extract, or even oysters themselves, in the brewing process. The first of these was produced by the Colchester Brewing Company, in England, around the end of the 19th century.

Pombo

Also known as **Pombé**, this is a sacred brew produced in Guinea, Africa, a millet-based beer to which herbs are added. The equivalents in neighbouring countries may also have bananas added to the mix.

Root Beer

A beer made using the roots of such plants as dandelion and sassafras. Today root beers are almost exclusively soft drinks (generally manufactured without any recourse whatsoever to roots), but traditionally they were fermented.

Rye Ale

Ale made using rye rather than barley as the grain; traditionally found wherever rye grew and beer was brewed, but most especially in the Baltic region. A few craft brewers today produce ales where some of the barley is replaced by rye; of longer establishment is the Bavarian brew **Schierlinger Roggenbier**.

Sahti

A traditional Finnish beer, often brewed to considerable strength (perhaps 12%) although more usually kept within normal beer ranges. The mixture uses straw, juniper branches and berries, with rye replacing some of the hops.

Sake

Although generally called rice wine, sake is technically more accurately described as a beer, since it is made from a cereal base – the cereal being, of course, rice. Sake is merely the strongest (with wine-like alcohol levels) and best known of a number of Japanese rice beers. Sake brewing is a process whose biochemistry is not yet fully understood.

Scotch Ale

Strong Scottish ales brewed primarily for export; the equivalent of the draught Heavies served in Scottish pubs as "90 shilling" (referring to the quondam price of a barrel of the brew).

Scottish Ale

Traditionally, beers brewed in Scotland during the preparation of which the malt was dried over peat fires, so the resulting brew had an interesting smoky flavour. Such luxuries are now largely a thing of the past; modern Scottish ales are distinguishable from their English counterparts largely through being sweeter, less hoppy and somewhat darker.

Sorghum Beers

Often referred to also as ***Bantu Beers*** or ***Kaffir Beers***, these thick African beers are brewed using sorghum, usually in a mixture with millet or corn, and generally drunk prior to full fermentation.

Spruce Beer

Beer made using the shoots of the red or black spruce in place of hops. These mild ales were popular in 17th-century North America.

Stingo
A very strong, malty ale brewed in Yorkshire and popular in its day, though relatively rarely seen now. A typical bottled Stingo would be not dissimilar to a Barley Wine in both affect and effect.

Tafelbier
A low-alcohol Flemish beer, known alternatively as ***Bière de Table*** among French-speaking consumers. It is produced by using previously utilized grains a second time.

Tsiou
A Chinese millet beer whose brewing can be traced back at least 4000 years. It is also drunk in an incompletely fermented style, and in this form is known as ***T'ien Tsiou***.

"Beer is proof that God loves us and wants us to be happy."
Benjamin Franklin

*"You can't be a real country unless you have a
beer and an airline – it helps if you have some kind of
a football team, or some nuclear weapons,
but at the very least you need a beer."*
Frank Zappa

*"They who get drunk on other intoxicating liquors fall
on all parts of their body; they fall on the left side,
on the right side, on their faces, and on their backs.
But those who get drunk on beer fall only on
their backs, and lie with their face upwards."*
Aristotle

A BEER CHARIVARI

Cerevisiology (n) The study of beer.
Cenosilicaphobia (n) Fear of an empty glass.

The word "beer" is said to derive ultimately from the Latin word *bibere*, "to drink", but this derivation seems suspect. In Old Norse – not a language strongly influenced by Latin – the word for "beer" was *bjorr* and in Old English it was *bēor*.

The expression "the hair of the dog" originated in a time when the best protection from a likely infectious dog bite was a belt of alcohol, the stronger the better.

The term "rule of thumb" comes from brewing. Before the advent of the thermometer, brewers tested the temperature of the mix prior to adding yeast by putting a thumb or finger into it; experience told them if the temperature was right.

The strongest beer ever made in the world (so far as is known) was first produced in the USA in 2001: Samuel Adams Utopias. The original brew weighed in at 24% alcohol, which meant it was edging toward the potency of spirits, and certainly well above fortified wines like sherry and port. Only 8000 bottles were made of this first batch, and any that are extant are now highly sought collectors' items. A further issue was made in 2003 that was even stronger, at 25% alcohol.

THE WORLD'S GREATEST BEER DRINKERS

According to 1999 figures produced by the Brewers'
Association of Japan, the top beer drinkers in the world are
the citizens of the Czech Republic. Here are the top 15 beer-
drinking countries in that year, with the figures for annual
beer consumption per capita in litres/Imperial pints/US
pints:

1	Czech Republic	160.7	282.7	339.1
2	Ireland	152.8	268.8	322.4
3	Germany	127.5	224.3	269.0
4	Austria	108.9	191.6	229.8
5	Luxembourg	106.6	187.5	224.9
6	Denmark	104.6	184.0	220.7
7	UK	99.0	174.1	208.9
8	Belgium	97.7	171.9	206.1
9	Australia	95.0	167.1	200.5
10	Slovakia	86.4	152.0	182.3
11	Netherlands	85.3	150.0	180.0
12	USA	84.4	148.5	178.1
13	New Zealand	84.0	147.8	177.2
14	Finland	80.1	140.1	169.0
15	Venezuela	75.7	133.2	159.7

A partial survey done in 2004 of European countries showed
that consumption in Denmark, Germany, Ireland and the
Netherlands dropped fairly sharply in the intervening years,
while in most other European countries the figure gently
rose.

    Similar national figures aren't available – or really mean-
ingful – at the lower end of the scale. However, the 2002
figures for the highest- and lowest-drinking US states are:

Nevada	184	324	388
Utah	79	139	167

Surveys done at the end of the 20th century on US beer-drinking habits threw up some interesting statistics:

❖ Less than half as many women as men drink beer – 17.2 million against 37 million – and those women who do drink beer drink only about half as much: 11.3 "servings" per month as opposed to 22.8.

❖ The drinking of imported beers is very much affected by demographics. Men aged 18–34 are 81% more likely than other aficionados to drink imports, while those with higher incomes (above $75,000) are over 50% more likely to. Those with college-degree or higher levels of education are 47% more likely to favour imports, while people over 65 are 60% more likely to stick to domestic beers.

❖ Drinkers claim to be largely unaffected in their choice of tipple by promotional efforts; either consumers are deceiving themselves or the big brewers are wasting huge amounts of money. Of the beer-drinkers surveyed, 88% said advertising didn't influence their choice of brand and 83% said in-store displays had no effect. When asked if they could remember seeing or hearing a beer advertisement in the previous month, only 59% of men responded positively and even fewer than that – 49% – of women.

The recognition by the RateBeer Best Awards of a beer as the best in the world would have spelled a commercial bonanza for just about any brewery whose brew had received the accolade, but not the winners of the Summer 2005 competition, the Trappist monks of the St Sixtus monastery in Flanders, Belgium. The winning beer, the brown ale Westvleteren Abt 12, was the premium of the three they brew; the others are Westvleteren 8 (also a brown ale, rated 22 in the world by RateBeer) and the light beer Westvleteren Blond (which is the only one the monks themselves are allowed to drink).

The Westvleteren beers have not been distributed commercially since 1941; the only place you can licitly buy them is at the monastery, where each customer is limited to five cases of 24 bottles (totalling 40 litres) and must promise not to resell them – although many break the promise, at considerable profit. The monastery's bottling plant can fill about 12,000 bottles per hour; total annual production, representing 70–75 days of brewing, is restricted to 4500 hectolitres.

The problem for the monks is that the purpose of their brewing activities is to make only as much money as is needed to finance their community; they have no desire whatsoever to capitalize on the accolade, and additional publicity is nothing but a nuisance for them.

Westvleteren Abt 12 has a 12% alcohol content, which puts it well into the wine range so far as potency is concerned.

Now an annual international bestseller, *The Guinness Book of Records* (the title has varied slightly over the years) is a household name; for a while it also served as the basis for a TV series. Its origins go back to 1951 when Sir Hugh Beaver, then the Managing Director of Guinness, got into an argument with a friend about game birds. It struck him that this was the kind of "debate" people constantly got into in pubs. A definitive reference book of trivial facts could surely serve a purpose in settling such controversies. The first edition of the book appeared in 1955, edited by Ross and Norris McWhirter.

STRANGE BREWS

Among the odder varieties of beer is Crop Circle Beer, made by various breweries on both side of the Atlantic from grain that has been flattened during the formation of crop circles, or at least from the fields in which crop circles have formed. Canadian farmer Dudley Cates claims to have been the first to come up with the notion, but may have been pre-empted by UK brewers like the Hop Back Brewery. As at least one cynic has

BEER MUSEUMS

Some beer museums around the world (with the sponsoring/
owning brewer where relevant and/or not obvious):

Alkmaar: De Boom National Beer Museum, Netherlands
Amsterdam: Heineken Museum, Netherlands
Baie Saint-Paul, Quebec: Charlevoix Microbrewery,
Canada
Boston, Massachusetts: Boston Beer Company Museum,
USA
Brussels: Brewery Museum, Belgium
Bury St Edmunds: Greene King Ale Museum, UK
Burton-on-Trent: Bass Museum, UK
Dublin: Guinness Storehouse, Ireland
Fort Worth, Texas: Brew Kettle Museum (Millers), USA
Kulmbach: Bavarian Brewery Museum, Germany
Madrid: Museo de la Cervesa, Spain
Milwaukee, Wisconsin: Museum of Beer & Brewing[1], USA
New Ulm, Minnesota: Schell's Beer Museum, USA
Plzen: The Brewery Museum (Pilsner Urquell),
Czech Republic
Pottsville, Pennsylvania: Yuengling Brewery, USA
Salzburg: Stiegl's Brauwelt, Austria
Sapporo: Sapporo Beer Museum, Japan
Toppenish, Washington State: American Hop Museum,
USA

[1] *Not yet open at time of writing, but expected to open imminently*

remarked, the popularity of the various beers may outlast the
popularity of crop circles . . .

At least one beer brand has come into existence because of a
running joke on radio. In the 1950s the Pittsburgh broadcaster
Rege Cordic had a lot of fun with the invented brand Ye Olde

Frothingslosh Pale Stale Ale, which was purportedly so light
that the beer floated on top of the froth: "A Whale of an Ale for
the Pale Stale Male" ran one of his invented radio ads for the
stuff. The Pittsburgh Brewing Co. latched onto the popularity of
the joke and began producing short runs of Olde Frothingslosh
(in fact, one of their established brews in an "Olde
Frothingslosh" can) for Christmas and other holiday consumption. There was even a fake Miss Olde Frothingslosh, whose
photo appeared tantalizingly on some of the cans – well, tantalizingly for fans of female heavyweight wrestling, that is.

Another curio for the connoisseur is Nessie's Monster Mash
Beer, made in Scotland (of course!) by the Cairngorm Brewery.

One of the oddest commercial brands is Nude Beer, manufactured in the USA. The website at www.drinknudebeer.com
coyly reveals no brewery name, but does claim that the beer won
a Gold Medal at the 1996 World Beer Cup. The beer's name
refers, of course, to how this is a pure, unadulterated beer, without any of the additives that have become near-universal in the
modern age, and has nothing at all to do with the fact that the
bottle has a special label which you can peel back to reveal a
topless photo of a pretty girl.

Yet another unusual brew is Bad Frog Beer. This owes its origin
to artist Jim Wauldron, who in 1994 was commissioned to
design a series of "bad animal" T-shirts. Most of the animals he
depicted looked fine, but everyone agreed the frog was a little
lacking, so he redrew the creature as a scowling beer-drinker
giving the viewer the (webbed) finger. The T-shirts sold well, and
inquiries came in as to where people could buy the beer to
match the design. This inspired Wauldron to set up his own
microbrewery, which now produces three Bad Frog beers, with
Bad Frog Golden Amber Lager the frontrunner. They can be
checked out at www.badfrog.com.

The beer Old Dusseldorf has the distinction of being famous though entirely fictional. It was the strongly preferred beer of Magnum (Tom Selleck) in the long-running TV show *Magnum P.I.*, but was available in only two bars on Hawaii – hence the focus on the beer, because Magnum had difficulty getting hold of it.

The favourite beer in the animated TV series *The Simpsons* is Duff Beer, and during the 1990s an Australian brewery briefly – before being stopped by the series' producers – obliged the demands of the marketplace by making and selling Duff Beer. In early 2005 an Australian woman was given 18 months' probation for attempting to sell cases of Duff Beer on eBay. Her crime wasn't selling the stuff. Quite the contrary: it was that she didn't actually have any Duff Beer to sell, her offers being purely fraudulent.

And another fictional brew is the Mexican beer Chongo. This first appeared in Robert Rodriguez's movie *Desperado* (1995) and returned in the same director's *From Dusk Till Dawn* the following year, in the latter movie being the beer on sale in the vampire bar. What gives Chongo its distinctive flavour, according to the bartender (Cheech Marin) in *Desperado*, is that the locals piss in it.

Not Just a Pretty Drink

Your spouse may not believe you when you patiently explain this on getting home late from the pub, but beer has definite curative properties, and holds the promise for more.

♦   Hops contain an antioxidant called xanthohumol which inhibits the growth of tumorous cells. Experiments are being done to create a special high-xanthohumol beer whose consumption could contribute to cancer prevention.

◆ It's long been known by the medical profession that moderate consumption of alcohol is good for the heart . . . and, although red wine is much touted, in fact beer is the best drink of all for this. Drinking a glass of beer each evening leads to about a 30% increase in the body's supply of vitamin B_6, a vitamin that's good for the heart. A glass of red wine, by contrast, elevates the B_6 levels by only about half this.

◆ The soluble fibre in beer can act to lower cholesterol, which again is useful in lowering the threat of heart failure.

◆ Beer consumption aids digestion and encourages bowel movements.

◆ Drinking beers rich in hops like porter or stout helps prevent the formation of kidney stones. And, if you're unlucky enough to suffer one of these, beer is as efficacious as the generally recommended cranberry juice in dilating the ureter so that the stone may be passed with less pain.

◆ Bottled and canned beers are good for settling upset stomachs, because of their carbonation. Of course, other fizzy drinks are carbonated as well, but the alcohol in beer gives it the added bonus of acting as a mild pain-killer.

◆ Regular moderate consumption of beer (or wine) throughout life leads to stronger bones in old age.

It would be theoretically possible to live on a diet consisting entirely of orange juice, milk and stout. That's the good news. The bad news is that the daily consumption of each of these three would have to be:

1 glass of orange juice
2 glasses of milk
22 litres (39 Imperial pints, 47 US pints) of stout

BEER AND YOUR LOW-CARB DIET

Beer and to a lesser extent other alcoholic drinks are often listed as anathema to the low-carb diets that have become so popular. However, most of the reasons given for the condemnation are spurious.

❖ Alcohol consumption does not increase levels of sugar in the blood. The end product of the liver's metabolic conversion of alcohol is acetate, not sugar. Drinking alcohol generally causes a *reduction* in blood sugar.

❖ Beer does not contain high levels of maltose (one of the sugars), as is often claimed.

❖ The Glycemic Index of alcoholic drinks is zero.

❖ All wines contain carbohydrates, even though we're often told that dry white wines are virtually carb-free.

❖ Non-alcoholic beer (Near Beer) is generally higher in carbs than real beer, sometimes having levels double that of the alcoholic variety. After all, the process of fermentation involves converting carbohydrates to alcohol . . .

❖ As an aside, rum does not contain higher levels of sugar than other distilled drinks, as is sometimes claimed in the low-carb diet plans; in fact, like them, it has zero sugar content. Although plenty of carbohydrates are present in the raw materials for distilled liquors, by the end of the distillation process those carbs have all been converted to ethyl alcohol.

HANGOVER CURES

Medics insist that the only effective ameliorative for a
hangover is a pain reliever combined with bed rest and the
drinking of copious quantities of water. Nevertheless, folk
remedies abound. Here are a few:

❖   Water – plenty of it. Most hangover remedies
    recommend this in addition to the rest. Some of the
    worst symptoms of hangover are caused by general
    dehydration of the body, and water is the best liquid
    with which to reverse this. One pre-emptive recom
    mendation is to drink lots of water before falling into
    bed; this has the effect of ensuring you get up several
    times during the night, when you can drink more
    water.

❖   The Ancient Greeks recommended eating raw cabbage.

❖   The Ancient Romans preferred fatty fried foods,
    with fried canaries being especially popular.

❖   A Bloody Mary. This concoction was invented in the
    1920s and comprises vodka (or gin), tomato juice
    and a seasoning like Tabasco Sauce.

❖   A Black Velvet, made by mixing Guinness and
    champagne.

❖   A Red Eye, made from whisky, orange juice, coffee,
    raw egg, Tabasco Sauce and pepper all popped in the
    blender together. But, if you're capable of preparing
    something more complex, you probably don't need a
    hangover cure.

❖   Beer and tomato juice – the recommendation of
    Ernest Hemingway.

❖   Buttermilk.

❖   Bananas. Bananas are a rich source of magnesium,
    which has the effect of relaxing the blood vessels.

❖   Coffee made with tonic water, honey and orange juice.

❖   Vitamin B-complex, vitamin C and/or vitamin E,
    complemented by plenteous water.

Stale beer left over after parties shouldn't be just poured down the sink but instead used in the garden as a fertilizer. Try to make sure you don't use beer that contains preservatives.

Another garden use of beer – preferably a beer like Bud rather than anything you might want to drink – is to control slugs and snails in the garden. Simply bury a jar (an old jamjar is fine) a few yards away from your flowerbeds so that the open top is at ground-level, fill it about three-quarters full with cheap beer, and let nature do the rest. The smell of the beer attracts the molluscs, who fall in and drown. Obviously you have to refresh your beer-trap fairly regularly, and cleaning it out can be somewhat revolting, but it works extremely well.

Beer makes an excellent hair conditioner . . . but not used straight from the glass, can or bottle. Boil the beer first to evaporate off the alcohol, and then, after it's cooled, mix it with the shampoo of your choice for use as a first-rate all-in-one shampoo–conditioner.

Because of its acidity, beer offers an efficacious way of cleaning metal and other surfaces – in fact, that's why we have beer mats: to *stop* unwanted removal by beer of the finishes of furniture. For a metal surface, just pour on beer, leave it a while, and then towel it off.

The six-pointed star that still features on many beer labels, and which was especially popular in the 19th and early 20th centuries, is known as the Brewers' Star. Its association with brewing can be traced back to the 13th century, when it was one of the religious icons with which brewers would bedizen their workplace to keep the Devil out of the brew (see page 21); by the 16th century it had come to be part of the official insignia of many traditional Brewers' Guilds. The six points of the star supposedly represent the essential ingredients used for beer: grain, hops, malt, water, yeast – and, of course, the brewer.

One mystery that remains unsolved is the origin of the prominently displayed number "33" that's appeared on the Rolling Rock label ever since the beer's launch in 1939. The company's files reveal no clue, so plentiful theories – and myths – have been promulgated:

♦ Prohibition for beer was repealed in 1933.
♦ The brewery was bought in 1933 using the proceeds of a $33 outside bet placed by one of the Tito family on a horse whose number was 33.
♦ In the brewery, 33 steps led up from the brewing floor to the brewmaster's office.
♦ 33 streams feed into the reservoir from which comes the water used in the making of the beer.
♦ The beer tastes best when drunk at 33°F, just above freezing point. Alternatively the beer was fermented at 33°F.
♦ There is a "pledge" that from the first has appeared on the back of the bottle that is 33 words long: "Rolling Rock. From the glass-lined tanks of Old Latrobe we tender this premium beer for your enjoyment, as a tribute to your good taste. It comes from the mountain springs to you."

The Tito family's explanation (they sold the brewery to Labatt in 1987) is that originally, back in the 1930s, there was hot debate over the wording of the pledge. Most of the suggestions were way too long. When one family member produced the version quoted above, he wrote a large "33" as a wordcount on the paper beneath it. The label's printer assumed the "33" was part of the copy, and accordingly typeset it. After the first batch of labels had been used up, the number could have been removed, but by then, well, if it ain't bust why fix it?

JOE'S RANT

One of the most successful ads in Canadian history was the celebrated "Joe's Rant", launched by Molson in early 2000 in cinemas and then graduating to TV, to promote their brand Molson Canadian. Voiced by a plaid-shirt-clad Mr Everyman in front of a montage of Canadian icons, it went:

> Hey! I'm not a lumberjack, or a fur trader.
> And I don't live in an igloo, or eat blubber, or own a dogsled.
> And I don't know Jimmy, Sally or Suzy from Canada, although I'm certain they're really, really nice.
> I have a Prime Minister, not a President.
> I speak English and French, *not* American, and I pronounce it "about", *not* "a boot".
> I can proudly sew my country's flag on my back pack. I believe in peacekeeping, *not* policing, diversity, *not* assimilation, and that the beaver is a truly proud and noble animal.
> A toque is a hat, a chesterfield is a couch, and it's pronounced "zed", not "zee" – "*zed*"!
> Canada is the second-largest landmass! The first nation of hockey! And THE BEST PART OF NORTH AMERICA!
> My name is Joe!
> And I am a *Canadian*!
> Thank you.

The rant was played at sporting events for the entertainment of the fans, who joined in with the words in an enormous, air-punching chorus. In bars people asked for the volume to be turned up whenever the ad came on air, so they could shout along with it. Rumours (false) abounded that the Minister of Consumer Affairs wanted to ban the ad for fear of a US backlash. But this staunch declaration of Canadian individuality lived on . . .

One of the more enticing religious sects is the Beer Church, whose website is to be found at www.beerchurch.com. You can join up easily as a congregant, and can even undergo a course of training to become a Beer Church Minister. Describing itself as "The Largest Unorganized Religion in the World", the church is a significant donor to charity and sums its philosophy up thus: "We are a loosely connected group of beer drinkers who are associated by our appreciation of beer. Christians have their faith in God and their love of Christ as a unifying factor that organizes or congregates them into a larger group. We have beer as our unifying factor. Beer Church does not mean to offend Christians or anyone else. As long as they are working to make the world a better place, we like everyone regardless of their opinion of beer or their opinion of us. Beer Church is not about worshipping beer. Beer is good. It is part of our social makeup. We hope to instill in people a sense of social responsibility that includes drinking responsibly. Join us in our mission. Dedicate yourself to making the world a better place one beer at a time. Be nice to people. Care about your community. Don't be offensive in your love of beer. Respect other people who have something different that they believe in or love. Be responsible and use beer as a way to do good things. That's all we ask."

The Beer Church has over 100,000 members, drawn from 26 different countries.

In 1988 a Canadian man was killed by exploding beer. He'd put his beer in the freezer compartment on top of his upright refrigerator. When he went to fetch himself a can, it exploded as he put his hand on it and erupted out of the freezer to hit him on the forehead with sufficient force to kill him.

Corporations often play dirty when struggling for a market share, but there have been few dirtier tricks than the one mounted in 1987 by the Reno company Luce & Sons, one of Heineken's distributors in the US, against the Mexican beer

Corona, which was eroding Heineken's US market share. According to the slur – which spread like wildfire – workers at Corona's Mexican breweries were urinating into the vats of the beer destined for US export (see the discussion of Chongo on page 59). Since Corona is of an appropriate colour, and since this colour is emphasized by the beer's clear bottles, it wasn't hard for the credulous to accept the lie as fact.

Luce settled the Corona lawsuit by publicly announcing that the rumour was entirely false, but it still cost the Mexican company over $500,000 in advertising and untold amounts in PR to repair the damage to its sales. Pleasingly, it's now the best-selling import beer in the US – ahead of Heineken.

In the late 1990s Anheuser–Busch, concerned about the fact that US women drink far less beer than their male counterparts, did a survey of women to find out what they wanted from a beer. Less gassiness, a more sophisticated image and a choice of strengths featured high among the preferences expressed. One suggestion that got a resounding thumbs-down was the market-ing of "chick beer" in pink bottles.

In summer 2005 it was reported that Cameroonians were using beer-bottle caps as currency. Rival breweries were using the ploy of giving away prizes to lucky buyers of their beer; only by buying the bottle could you find the information printed on the underside of the cap telling you if you'd won. The rarer prizes included cars and mobile phones; a more common prize was further bottled beer. Over 20 million bottles of beer were given away in prizes, but not always to the original purchaser of the lucky beer. Since a bottle of beer cost about $1, the winning caps could be used as currency – and often were.

"The church is near but the road is icy.
The bar is far away but I will walk carefully."
Russian Proverb

THE PHANTOM BEER DRINKER: URBAN LEGENDS

While driving in the Tatra Mountains, Slovakian tourist Richard Kral was buried by an avalanche. He got the car window open and tried to dig his way out, but the snow was falling faster than he could drink. At last inspiration struck. For his holiday he'd brought with him five cases (60 half-litre bottles) of beer; if he could urinate copiously enough, he could melt his way out of this. Rescuers found him four days later staggering along a mountain path. "It was hard, and now my kidneys and liver hurt," he said once coherent, but at least he was alive.

The story was widely reported in the international press but seems to have been entirely invented.

In Japan in the mid-1990s, the Asaka Brewing Co. launched its revolutionary new Suiso beer, in which some of the carbon dioxide that forms the bubbles was replaced by hydrogen. The brew became popular in Japanese karaoke bars: sounds are pitched higher in a hydrogen atmosphere, so males could sing soprano parts after a few gulps of Suiso. In addition, of course, they could seemingly breathe blue fire by the simple expedient of belching across a lit cigarette. Sales of Suiso soared, but finally stalled when a drinker who'd badly injured himself trying the latter trick sued Asaka.

Unfortunately, there's no such stuff as hydrogen beer, or a brand called Suiso, or indeed an Asaka Brewing Co. . . .

Plenty of people have noticed that the exhaust pipe on the 2002 Mini Cooper looks a lot like a beer can. The story goes that one of the design teams, the night before the presentation of their design, was celebrating in the usual fashion when a team member spotted that they'd forgotten to put an exhaust pipe on their model. Quick as a flash, someone grabbed one of the empty beer cans and stuck it on the back of the model; a few dabs of paint and the design had an exhaust pipe. The team was successful at the presentation, and so they left the tail-pipe the way it was.

Before being bought by Pabst in 1999, the Rainier Brewery, bearing a huge red "R" in neon atop the building, was a Seattle landmark, but back in the 1930s it was the centre of a nasty controversy based on an urban legend. There had been heated local debate about the name of Seattle's most famous mountain. The citizens of Tacoma wanted to call it Mount Tacoma; others preferred Mount Rainier. Finally, Mount Rainier was the name selected, and promptly the rumours raged that the brewery had bribed Congress – with free beer, of course – to rule accordingly in order to give the brewery a massive and persisting dose of publicity.

In fact, the US Board of Geographic Names had determined as early as 1890 that the mountain was called Mount

Rainier. In the 1920s Congress debated a name-change to Mount Tacoma, but the debate went nowhere. All of this happened before 1933, when Prohibition ended and Emil Sick revived the brewery, naming it after the local mountain. But the legend still survives in Seattle that things were the other way round.

An urban legend, possibly started by a rival, did grave damage to the business of the Lone Star Brewery in San Antonio, Texas, during the winter of 1966-7. According to the tale, the decomposed remains of a murdered worker had been found in one of the vats, the man's hands having been cut off before he was thrown in so that he had no means of escape.

This legend is a variant of a whole family of such legends that can be traced back well over a century and still pop up from time to time: a worker either falls into or is killed and thrown into a vat of something edible or potable – wine, Coca-Cola, tomato juice, you name it – and the truth isn't discovered until the substance concerned has been widely consumed by the public.

Beer "Cocktails"

As any aficionado will tell you, there's absolutely no need to adulterate a good beer with anything else: it's perfect just the way it is. Nonetheless, over the centuries people have come up with various beer-based mixed drinks, some simple and some elaborate. Some of the older and more complicated recipes probably originated as a means of using up not-so-good or merely undistinguished beer – much in the same way as in the popular drink "lager and a dash", or "lager top", whereby bland commercial lager is given a little lift by the addition of a small quantity (up to about 10%) of what in the UK is called lemonade and in the US is called Seven-Up.

Aleberry
The original term was *ale bree*, meaning "ale broth". This is an ancient drink made by mixing hot ale, honey, sugar, toast and spices – a sort of mulled ale, in other words.

Ale Flip
Not everyone's cup of beer, this consists of ale, crushed ice and a raw egg – shaken, not stirred. Sounds almost as grim as a hangover cure . . .

Black and Tan
A half-and-half mixture of any dark beer with a light one; the British forces in Ireland during the 1920s were named after the drink, not the other way round. Suitable pairings are stout with bitter and porter with lager.

Black Velvet

A half-and-half mixture of champagne with stout, the stout being carefully added after the champagne down the inside of the glass so that the two liquids mix as little as possible. As for quantities, this is usually served in a champagne glass rather than a beer mug . . .

Cock Ale

This was a popular drink in 18th-century England; the preparation may be a little elaborate for the average beer drinker today. You will need:

- 12 gallons of ale
- 4 pounds of raisins
- 8 ounces of dates
- 1 quart of Canary
- 1 pint of yeast
- 2 ounces of mace and nutmeg
- a good-sized chicken

Soak the dates and the spices in the Canary for a day. Boil the chicken in a gallon of water until the meat more or less jellifies and the gallon has reduced to a half-gallon of stock, then press the meat until the last of the liquid comes out of it, adding this to the stock. Put the stock, the soaked fruit and some extra mace in the ale along with a pint of yeast. Your Cock Ale should be ready for drinking in a couple of days – sooner in hot weather.

Egg Ale

Another complicated concoction from English history that only the most dedicated and resourceful home-brewer might want to try. You will need:

- a dozen raw eggs
- the gravy of 8 pounds of beer

- 1 pound of raisins
- 1 orange, whole, segmented
- spices to taste
- a 12-gallon barrel of ale just started fermenting
- 2 quarts of Malaga Sack

Lightly stir together the raw eggs and put them with the gravy, raisins, orange segments and spices in a linen bag. Tie off the linen bag and put it in the barrel of ale. Once the ale has finished fermenting, add the Sack and leave for about three weeks. Bottle, adding a little sugar to prime.

Lambswool

In medieval England the first day of November was called La Mas Ubal, meaning "Day of the Apple"; it was a Christianized fertility festival. The name was corrupted to Lambswool, and this word was also applied to the mulled ale traditionally concocted for it. You will need:

- 2 pints strong ale
- 6 roasted apples
- 1 grated nutmeg
- 1 pinch ginger
- sugar to taste

Heat the ale to about the temperature of mulled wine, then stir in the other ingredients, adding extra sugar as required. Serve as you would mulled wine or hot punch.

Mild and Bitter

Exactly what the name implies: half a pint of draught mild ale mixed with half a pint of bitter. This is a refreshing summer drink that, if you're lucky with the pairing, brings out the best in both beers, the bitterness of the bitter countering the sweetness of the mild so that the latter's flavour is allowed more fully to present itself.

Scurvy-Grass Ale

Before the true cause of scurvy was discovered, this had wide-spread regard as a preventative and cure for the disease. To ale was added an infusion of watercress.

Shandy

Traditionally this was a mixture of ale and ginger. In due course it became a half-and-half mixture of ale (preferably English bitter) and ginger beer; later ginger ale became a viable alternative to ginger beer. Today it is generally a mixture of either ale or lager with what the British call lemonade, the Americans Seven-Up; discerning drinkers, however, still opt for a shandy made with ginger beer and bitter. It's an ideal summer and sporting drink, since it supplies liquid and sugar without the full complement of alcohol.

Tewadiddle

A traditional English beer-based drink: to a pint of ale add a tablespoonful of brandy, a little brown sugar, a few thin strips of lemon rind, and nutmeg and/or ginger to taste.

Wassail

A drink that gave its name to the Christmas practice of wassailing; "wassail" derives from the Old Norse drinking toast *ves heill*, meaning "be in health". Wassailers would go from house to house bearing a bowl of wassail, which was warm spiced ale prepared to various recipes. The first formalized version was created before 1732 by one Sir Watkin W. Wynne, who in that year presented the huge wassail bowl he had made to Jesus College, Oxford. For his recipe you will need a large bowl and:

- 1 pound sugar
- 1 pint ale, warmed
- grated ginger and nutmeg to taste
- 4 glasses sherry
- 5 further pints of ale
- sugar to taste
- 4 slices of toast
- a sliced lemon

Put the sugar in the bowl and pour the pint of warm ale over it. Add the sherry and the ginger/nutmeg, then stir. Add the remaining ale, stir again, taste, and add sugar if desired. Leave covered for three or four hours. Float the toast on the liquid. Immediately before serving, add the slices of lemon.

*"Fill with mingled cream and amber,
I will drain that glass again.
Such hilarious visions clamber
Through the chambers of my brain.
Quaintest thoughts, queerest fancies
Come to life and fade away;
What care I how time advances?
I am drinking ale today."*
Edgar Allan Poe

FESTIVALS OF BEER

New beer festivals are constantly being born as old ones, sadly, die, but the number of beer festivals worldwide appears to be steadily – indeed, rapidly – increasing, especially in the UK.

So far as enthusiasts are concerned, the seeming purpose of beer festivals differs between the two sides of the Atlantic. On the European side, the tasting is done using half-pint, pint or half-litre glasses. Charitably, one might say that, since beer is intended to refresh as well as fortify, it can only be fully appreciated in quantity; less charitably, one can assume that most attendees would like to drink a lot of beer.

On the North American side of the ocean, attendees are more typically issued on arrival with a tasting glass of capacity two fluid ounces, or even one fluid ounce. While this enables far more beers to be sampled before, um, the enthusiast's critical discernment becomes deleteriously impaired, it's a moot point as to whether a beer can properly be assessed with a single gulp.

═══ SOME NOTABLE BEER FESTIVALS ═══

American Institute of Wine & Food Beer & Food Fest
Held annually since 1990, usually in mid-March, in Lower Manhattan, New York City. A unique feature of this festival is the teaming up of celebrated New York chefs with individual microbreweries to produce inspired pairings of dishes with particular beers.

Boston Brewers' Festival
Held annually since 1992, usually in May, at the World Trade Center in Boston, Massachusetts.

California Beer Festival
Held annually since 1995, usually in April, in San Diego. There are two contests: a People's Choice Award, judged by attendees, and a Best of Show, judged by a panel.

Cannstatter Wasen Volksfest
Established in 1818 in Stuttgart by the King of Württemberg and held annually since then, usually in September/October at about the same time as Munich's Oktoberfest.

Scottish Traditional Beer Festival
Held annually by CAMRA in June at the Meadowbank Stadium in Edinburgh.

Frühjahrs Starkbierfest
A seventeen-day festival held annually in March/April, beginning on St Joseph's Day (March 19), in Munich; the focus is on strong beers (*starkbiers*), especially doppelbocks.

Great American Beer Festival
Held annually since 1981 in Denver, Colorado, this is North America's biggest beer festival. Prior to the festival there is a judged competition in 34 style categories, with Gold, Silver and Bronze medals being awarded in each.

Great British Beer Festival
Held annually in London (at Olympia) in August by CAMRA, this is the UK's biggest beer festival and has been operating since 1978; imports are featured as well as indigenous beers. Awards are given in several categories by a panel of judges, and there is also an overall Champion Beer of Britain (see page 95).

Great Canadian Beer Festival
Held annually in Victoria, British Columbia, in September, this is sponsored by the Canadian branch of CAMRA and attracts breweries – especially microbreweries – from all over the Western Seaboard of not just Canada but the northern USA.

Great Japan Beer Festival
Held annually in Tokyo in June or late May at the Yebisu Garden Palace in Tokyo, this was founded in 1998 by the Japan Craft Beer Association and the NPO Beer Taster Organization, and annually attracts about 30,000 enthusiasts to sample some 80 national and international brews. As with US beer festivals, the sampling is done with a small (50cc) glass.

Great Taste of the Midwest
Held annually in August in Madison, Wisconsin, since 1985, this relatively small festival attracts brewers and aficionados from all over the US Midwest.

Munich Oktoberfest
The most prestigious of all beer festivals, held annually since its inauguration in 1810 as part of the wedding celebrations for Crown Prince Ludwig (later King Ludwig I of Bavaria) and the Princess Therese of Saxe–Altenburg–Hildburghausen. The festival runs for the two weeks leading up to the first Sunday in October. Unlike many other beer festivals, this one does not invite participant breweries internationally or even nationally, instead being restricted to the handful that operate within the city limits: Augustiner, Hacker–Pschorr, Hofbräu, Lowenbräu, Paulaner and Spaten.

Poperinge Hoppestoet
Held in September every third year since 1956 in Poperinge, in Belgium, this festival of beer and hops is one of the few still surviving in Belgium, and lasts a week, with much pageantry and beer-drinking.

Rock, Rhythm & Brews
A charity festival of beer and live music held annually in October in Newport, Oregon. Over a hundred brews are available at the weekend-long festival, and the musical acts are generally major headliners; not surprising that upward of 10,000 fans turn up annually.

Traquair House Beer Festival

Held annually in late May at the Traquair House brewery in Inverleithen, Scotland. Traquair House has established an enviable reputation as a producer of some of the UK's very finest beers, and these are highlighted at the festival.

World Beer Games

Not strictly a beer festival, but a celebration of beer – and the associated camaraderie – focusing on six officially designated games: Beer Trivia, Boat Race, Empty Can Toss, Pint Chug, Pint Curl and Quarters. The medals in each event are designated – rather than the traditional Gold, Silver and Bronze – Lager, White and Ale. The Games are governed by the World Beer Games Sanctioning Body, which has issued a Code of Ethics and other rules; responsibility is a key issue, as in the Empty Can Toss contest, where the toss is into a recycling bin. At the inaugural event in 2002 in Toronto, Canada, there were teams from 16 countries: Barbados, Belgium, Canada, Dominican Republic, England, Greece, Guyana, Ireland, Italy, Jamaica, Philippines, Poland, Portugal, South Korea, Trinidad & Tobago, and the USA. For more details consult their website at www.worldbeergames.org.

"The mouth of a perfectly happy man is filled with beer."
Egyptian Proverb

"A fine beer may be judged with only one sip, but it's better to be thoroughly sure."
Czech Proverb

═══ BEER FESTIVAL CALENDAR ═══

The precise dates on which any beer festival is held vary from year to year, of course; here we locate the festivals to the approximate month. (In particular, festivals held in association with Easter vary in their month from one year to the next.) For more accurate dates in any particular year, consult www.ratebeer.com and www.camra.org.uk.

January
National Winter Ales Festival, UK
Anchorage: Great Alaska Beer & Barley Wine Festival, USA
Atherton Beer Festival (Bent & Bongs Beer Bash), UK
Burton-on-Trent Winter Ales Festival, UK
Cambridge Winter Ale Festival, UK
Chelmsford Winter Beer Festival, UK
Derby Winter Beer Festival, UK
Exeter Festival of Winter Ales, UK
Patchogue: Long Island Real Ale Festival, USA
Scottsdale Strong Beer Festival, USA

February
Ashfield Winter Beer Festival, UK
Battersea Beer Festival, UK
Bradford Beer Festival, UK
Chesterfield Beer Festival, UK
Dorchester Beer Festival, UK
Eugene, Oregon: KLCC Northwest Microbrew Festival, USA
Fleetwood Beer Festival, UK
Gosport Winter Beer Festival, UK
Hucknall Beer Festival, UK
Liverpool Beer Festival, UK
Nynäshamn Real Ale Festival, Sweden
Pasadena, California: Belgian Beer Festival, USA
Pendle Beer Festival, UK
Salisbury Winterfest, UK
Stockton Beer Festival, UK

Tewkesbury Winter Ale Festival, UK
White Cliffs Festival of Winter Ales, UK

March
Boulder, Colorado: Strong Ale Festival, USA
Bristol Beer Festival, UK
Burlington: Pepperwood Beer Festival, Canada
Coventry City Beer Festival, UK
Dunstable Beer Festival, UK
Ely: Elysian Beer Festival, UK
Hitchin Beer & Cider Festival, UK
Hove: Sussex Beer & Cider Festival, UK
Kailua–Kona, Hawaii: Kona Brewers' Fest, USA
Leeds Beer, Cider & Perry Festival, UK
Leicester Beer Festival, UK
London Drinker Beer & Cider Festival, UK
Loughborough Beer Festival, UK
Munich: Frühjahrs Starkbierfest, Germany
Newton Abbot: South Devon Beer Festival, UK
New York City: American Institute of Wine & Food Beer & Food Fest, USA
Peoria (Illinois) International Beer Festival, USA
Portland, Oregon: Spring Beer & Wine Fest, USA
Seattle: Barleywine Bacchanal, USA

Seattle: Spring Beer Festival (Hops on the Equinox), USA

Sint-Niklaas: Zythios Beer Festival, Belgium

Wigan Beer Festival, UK

York Beer Festival, UK

April

Baltimore: City Paper Beer Fest, USA

Banbury Beer Festival, UK

Bury St Edmunds: East Anglian Beer Festival, UK

Chippenham Beer Festival, UK

Farnham Beer Exhibition, UK

Fife Beer Festival, UK

Helsinki Beer Festival, Finland

Maldon Beer Festival, UK

Mansfield Beer & Cider Festival, UK

Newcastle Beer Festival, UK

Oldham Beer Festival, UK

Paisley Beer Festival, UK

Penticton, British Columbia: Okanagan Fest-of-Ale, Canada

Peoria, Arizona: Spring Hop Festival, USA

Philadelphia: Annual Brew Extravaganza, USA

Phoenix: Great Arizona Beer Festival, USA

Reading Beer & Cider Festival, UK

San Diego: California Beer Festival,USA

San Francisco International Beer Festival, USA

Scottsdale: Southwest Festival of Beers, USA

Seattle: Hard Liver Barleywine Festival, USA

Stourbridge Beer Festival, UK

Walsall Beer Festival, UK

Wear Valley Beer Festival, UK

May

Alloa Mayfest Ale Festival, UK

Austin: Texas Craft Brewers' Festival, USA

Barrow Hill Roundhouse Rail Ale Festival, UK

Boonville (California) Beer Fest, USA

Boston Brewers' Festival, USA

Brooklyn, NYC: Cask Ale Festival (Cask Head), USA

Calgary's International Beer Festival, Canada

Cambridge Beer Festival, UK

Chester Charity Beer Festival, UK

Colchester Real Ale & Cider Festival, UK

Frankenmuth, Michigan: World Expo of Beer, USA

Halifax Beer Festival, UK

Inverleithen: Traquair House Beer Festival, UK

Lincoln Beer Festival, UK

Macclesfield Beer Festival, UK

Maitland: Sunshine Challenge & Florida Craft Beer Festival, USA

Milwaukee: World of Beer Festival, USA

Naugatuck: Connecticut Brewers' Craft Beer Festival, USA

Newark Beer Festival, UK

Norfolk: Virginia Beer Festival, USA

Rugby CAMRA Beer Festival, UK

St Louis Microfest, USA

Sour & Bitter in Stockholm, Sweden

Tokyo: Great Japan Beer Festival, Japan

Yapton BeerEx, UK

June

Calgary Real Ale Festival, Canada

Catford Beer Festival, UK

Cheyenne: Wyoming Brewers' Festival, USA

Doncaster Beer Festival, UK

Ealing: Beer on Broadway Festival, UK

Edinburgh: Scottish Traditional Beer Festival, UK

Fort Collins: Colorado Brewers' Fest, USA

Hereford Beer & Cider Festival (Beer on the Wye), UK

Idaho Falls, Idaho: Mountain Brewers' Beer Fest, USA

Kingston-upon-Thames: Kingston Beer Festival, UK
Lausanne: Fête de la Bière, Switzerland
Lewes: South Downs & Cider Beer Festival, UK
Minneapolis: City Pages Beer Festival, USA
Montréal: Mondial de la Bière, Canada
Pittsburgh: Great European Beerfest, USA
St Ives Beer Festival, UK
Southampton Beer Festival, UK
Stockport Beer & Cider Festival, UK
Thurrock Beer Festival, UK
Tokyo: Japan Craft Beer Festival, Japan
Wolverhampton Beer Festival, UK
Woodchurch: Rare Breeds Beer Festival, UK

July

Boston Beer Festival, UK
Boxmoor Beer Festival, UK
Bromsgrove Beer Festival, UK
Burlington: Vermont Brewers' Festival, USA
Canterbury: Kent Beer Festival, UK
Chelmsford Beer Festival, UK
Cologne: Kölner Bierbörse, Germany
Derby Beer Festival, UK
Devizes Beer Festival, UK
Keystone, Colorado: Bluegrass & Beer Festival, USA
Plymouth Beer Festival, UK
Portland, Oregon: Portland International Beer Festival, USA
Queidersbach: Hahnenfest, Germany
Salisbury Summerfest, UK
San Francisco: KQED International Beer & Food Festival, USA
Seattle International Beer Festival, USA
Winchcombe: Cotswold Beer Festival, UK
Woodcote Festival of Ales, UK
Worcester, Massachusetts: Wachusett Summer Brew Fest, USA

August

Adamstown, Pennsylvania: Great Eastern Invitational Microbrewery Festival, USA
Berlin: Internationales Berliner Bierfestival, Germany
Clacton-on-Sea Beer Festival, UK
Dayton, Ohio: Ale Fest Dayton, USA
Flagstaff, Arizona: Made in the Shade Beer Tasting Festival, USA
Grass Valley, California: Sierra BrewFest, USA
Hayward, California: Beer Fest, USA
London: Great British Beer Festival, UK
Madison, Wisconsin: Great Taste of the Midwest, USA
Mammoth (California) Festival of Beers & Bluesapalooza, USA
Mumbles Beer Festival, UK
Peterborough Beer Festival, UK
Rochester, New York State: Flower City Brewers' Fest, USA
Seattle: Brouwers' Hopfest, USA
Toronto's Festival of Beer, Canada
Vancouver Caskival, Canada
Worcester Beer & Cider Festival, UK

September

Abergavenny Beer Festival, UK
Bagthorpe Beer Festival, UK
Birmingham Beer Festival, UK
Boston Oktoberfest, USA
Carmarthen Beer Festival, UK
Chambly, Québec: La Fête Bières & Saveurs, Canada
Chappel Beer Festival, UK
Darlington Beer & Music Festival (Rhythm'n'Brews), UK
Davenport, Iowa: Brew Ha Ha, USA
Denver: Great American Beer Festival, USA
Durham Beer Festival, UK
Glossop Victorian Weekend Beer Festival, UK
Harbury Beer Festival, UK

Harrisburg, Pennsylvania: Capital City Invitational Beer Festival, USA

Holyoke: Connecticut River Brewers' Festival, USA

Ipswich Beer Festival, UK

Keighley Beer, Cider & Perry Festival, UK

Letchworth Garden City Beer & Cider Festival, UK

Maidstone Beer & Hop Festival, UK

Melton Mowbray Beer Festival, UK

Minehead: Somerset Beer Festival, UK

Nantwich Beer Festival, UK

Northwich Beer Festival, UK

Oneida, New York State: Madison County Hop Fest, USA

Poperinge Hoppestoet[2], Belgium

St Albans Beer Festival, UK

St Ives: Booze on the Ouse Beer Festival, UK

Saltaire Beer Festival, UK

Scunthorpe Beer Festival, UK

Shrewsbury Real Ale Festival, UK

Solihull & District Beerfest, UK

Southport: Sandgrounder Beer Festival, UK

Superior, Wisconsin: Big Lake Brewfest, USA

Tamworth Beer Festival, UK

Telluride (Colorado) Blues & Brews Festival, USA

Troon: Ayrshire Real Ale Festival, UK

Ulverston Beer Festival, UK

Victoria: Great Canadian Beer Festival, Canada

Westford, Massachusetts: Blues & Brews Festival, USA

Whitehaven Beer Festival, UK

Worksop: North Notts Beer Festival, UK

[2] *Held every third year*

October

Barnsley CAMRA Beer Festival, UK

Bedford Beer & Cider Festival, UK

Bloomington, Indiana: Big Beer Festival, USA

Dunfermline Charity Beer Festival, UK

Durham, North Carolina: Annual World Beer Festival, USA

Eastbourne Beer Festival, UK

Gravesend Beer Festival, UK

Hull Real Ale & Cider Festival, UK

Kitchener & Waterloo, Ontario: Oktoberfest, Canada

Minneapolis Brew Review, USA

Munich Oktoberfest, Germany

Newport, Oregon: Rock, Rhythm & Brews, USA

Nottingham CAMRA Beer & Cider Festival, UK

Poole Beer Festival, UK

Portland: Oregon Cask Beer Festival, USA

Stockholm Beer Festival, Sweden

Stuttgart: Cannstatter Wasen Volksfest, Germany

Wakefield Beer Festival, UK

Weymouth Octoberfest, UK

Worthing Beer Festival, UK

November

Aberdeen & North East Beer Festival, UK

Milwaukee: Metro Kiwani's Brew Fest, USA

Mexico City Oktoberfest, Mexico

Nynäshamn Svartölsfestival, Sweden

Sandiacre: Erewash Valley Annual Beer Festival, UK

Woking Beer Festival, UK

December

Essen: Kerstbierenfestival, Germany

Oakland, California: Tasting of Holiday Beers, USA

Portland, Oregon: Holiday Ale Festival, USA

Toronto: Fall Beerfest, Canada

KEEP WATCHING THE BARS: BEER AWARDS

THE RATE BEER AWARDS

RateBeer (www.ratebeer.com) is a vast internet archive of beer ratings – over half a million ratings from all over the world. Its semi-annual craft beer competition is judged by thousands of beer enthusiasts worldwide; for the Summer 2005 Awards there were over 30,000 beers entered by over 4000 brewers in 120 countries.

The Summer 2005 top 100 RateBeer Best Award winners worldwide were:

1	Westvleteren Abt 12 (Belgium)
2	Three Floyds Dark Lord Russian Imperial Stout (USA)
3	Bells Expedition Stout Imperial Stout (USA)
4	Kuhnhenn Raspberry Eisbock (USA)
5	AleSmith Speedway Stout (USA)
6	Nørrebro Bryghus North Bridge Extreme (Denmark)
7	Rochefort Trappistes 10 (Belgium)
8	Three Floyds Dreadnaught Imperial IPA (USA)
9	Stone Imperial Russian Stout (USA)
10	Oggis Hop Whompus (USA)
11	AleSmith Barrel Aged Old Numbskull (USA)
12	AleSmith YuleSmith India Pale Ale (USA)
13	Founders Breakfast Stout (USA)
14	Pizza Port Frank Double IPA (USA)
15	Thirsty Dog Siberian Night Imperial Stout (USA)
16	Southampton Imperial Russian Stout (USA)
17	Pannepot (Belgium)
18	St Bernardus Abt 12 (Belgium)

19   Dogfish Head World Wide Stout (USA)
20   Pizza Port Cuvee de Tomme (USA)
21   Flossmoor Station Imperial Eclipse Stout (USA)
22   Westvleteren Extra 8 (Belgium)
23   Victory Storm King Imperial Stout (USA)
24   Goose Island Bourbon County Stout (USA)
25   Apis Póstorak Jadwiga Mead (Poland)
26   Town Hall Czar Jack Imperial Stout (USA)
27   Central Waters Brewers Reserve Bourbon (USA)
28   New Glarus Belgian Red (USA)
29   Rochefort Trappistes 8 (Belgium)
30   Pizza Port Santa's Little Helper (USA)
31   Barley Johns Dark Knight Imperial Porter (USA)
32   Double Bastard Ale (USA)
33   Andechser Doppelbock Dunkel (Germany)
34   Free State Owd Mac's Imperial (USA)
35   Great Divide Oak Aged Yeti Imperial Stout (USA)
36   Great Divide Hercules Double IPA (USA)
37   Kuhnhenn Fourth Dementia Old Ale (USA)
38   Southampton Abbot 12 (USA)
39   AleSmith Old Numbskull (USA)
40   North Coast Old Rasputin Russian Imperial Stout
     (USA)
41   Abbaye des Rocs Brune (Belgium)
42   Free State Old Backus Barleywine (USA)
43   Dogfish Head 90 Minute Imperial IPA (USA)
44   Dieu du Ciel Péché Mortel (Canada)
45   Bush Prestige (Belgium)
46   Eylenbosch Framboise Cuvee Speciale (Belgium)
47   Town Hall Wee Heavy (USA)
48   Cidrerie Léo Boutin Pomelle (Cider) (Canada)
49   Stone Ruination IPA (USA)
50   Abbaye des Rocs Grand Cru (Belgium)
51   New Glarus Raspberry Tart (USA)
52   Founders Imperial Stout (USA)
53   Bells Kalamazoo Stout (USA)
54   Victory Old Horizontal (USA)

55	Dogwood Youngbloods Imperial Porter (USA)
56	Drafting Room 10th Anniversary Ale (USA)
57	AleSmith IPA (USA)
58	Marin Eldridge Grade White Knuckle Double IPA (USA)
59	Great Divide Yeti Imperial Stout (USA)
60	Dominion Oak Barrel Aged Millennium (USA)
61	Ayinger Celebrator Doppelbock (Germany)
62	Fullers London Porter (England)
63	Third Coast Old Ale (USA)
64	New Belgium La Folie (USA)
65	J.W. Lees Harvest Ale (England)
66	AleSmith J.P. Grays Wee Heavy Scotch Ale (USA)
67	Hair of the Dog Adam (USA)
68	Hair of the Dog Doggie Claws 2003-04 (USA)
69	Abbaye des Rocs Triple Impériale (Belgium)
70	Barley Johns Barrel Aged Rosie's Ale (USA)
71	Southern Tier Imperial Oatmeal Stout (USA)
72	Nynäshamns Fatlagrad Smörpundet Porter (Sweden)
73	Iron Hill Russian Imperial Stout (USA)
74	Brooklyn Black Chocolate Stout (USA)
75	Schneider Aventinus (Germany)
76	La Bavaisienne (France)
77	Pizza Port SPF 45 Saison (USA)
78	Pizza Port Lou P. Lin (USA)
79	Three Floyds Alpha Klaus Christmas Porter (USA)
80	Dupont Avec Les Bons Voeux (Belgium)
81	Rogue Chocolate Stout (USA)
82	Arrogant Bastard Ale (USA)
83	St Ambroise Oatmeal Stout (Canada)
84	AleSmith Grand Cru (USA)
85	Three Floyds Alpha King (USA)
86	Two-Hearted Ale (USA)
87	Drie Fonteinen Oude Geuze (Belgium)
88	McNeill's Imperial Stout (USA)
89	McKenzie Avec Les Bons Voeux (USA)
90	Terrapin Big Hoppy Monster (USA)

91	Sly Fox Simcoe IPA (USA)
92	Town Hall Masala Mama IPA (USA)
93	LaConner India Pale Ale (Bottleworks) (USA)
94	Bièropholie Impérial Stout (Canada)
95	Stone India Pale Ale (USA)
96	Girardin Gueuze Black Label (Belgium)
97	Gouden Carolus Cuvee Van De Keizer (Belgium)
98	Rogue Imperial Stout (USA)
99	Crouch Vale Brewers Gold Extra (England)
100	De Dolle Oerbier Special Reserva (Belgium)

RateBeer National Ratings

The Summer 2005 RateBeer Best Awards for the best beers by country were:

Belgium
1	De Dolle Stille Nacht Reserva
2	Westvleteren Abt 12
3	Drie Fonteinen Framboos
4	Rochefort Trappistes 10
5	De Dolle Speciaal Brouwsel 20
6	St Bernardus Abt 12
7	Pannepot
8	Westvleteren Extra 8
9	Rochefort Trappistes 8
10	Belle-Vue Sélection Lambic

Canada
1	Dieu du Ciel Péché Mortel
2	Cidrerie Léo Boutin Pomelle
3	St Ambroise Oatmeal Stout
4	Bièropholie Impérial Stout
5	Unibroue Trois Pistoles
6	Fat Cat Old Bad Cat Barley Wine
7	Unibroue Quelque Chose
8	Unibroue Maudite

9   Unibroue La Fin Du Monde
10   Dieu du Ciel Grande Noirceur

Czech Republic
1   Herold Cerny Lezák 13%
2   Pardubický Porter (Boom)
3   Herold Svetlé
4   Herold Pulnocni Psenicne
5   Bernard 13% Cerne
6   Pilsner Urquell
7   Lobkowicz Baron
8   Herold Psenicne (Hefeweizen)
9   Staropramen Kelt Original Stout
10   Budweiser Budvar Tmavý Lexák

Denmark
1   Nørrebro Bryghus North Bridge Extreme
2   Wintercoat Double Hop
3   Wintercoat Cockney Imperial Stout
4   Vikingernes Mjød Dansk Mjød
5   Thisted Limfjords Porter/Double Brown Stout
6   Grauballe Nørrebryg
7   Ølbutikken IPA
8   Brøckhouse Juleøl
9   Carlsberg Carls Porter (Gammel Carlsberg
        Porter/Imperial Stout)
10   Grauballe Barley Wine

England
1   J.W. Lees Harvest Ale
2   Crouch Vale Brewers Gold Extra
3   Thomas Hardy's Ale (vintage 2003 and later)
4   Freeminer Deep Shaft Stout
5   Darwin Rolling Hitch
6   Dark Star Critical Mass
7   Greene King Strong Suffolk (Old Ale)
8   J.W. Lees Harvest Ale (Lagavulin)

9	Theakstons Old Peculier (Cask)
10	J.W. Lees Harvest Ale (Sherry)

France

1	La Bavaisienne
2	Cidre Dupont Réserve
3	St Sylvestre Bière Nouvelle
4	La Choulette Ambrée
5	Etienne Dupont Cidre Bouché Brut de Normandie
6	La Choulette de Noël
7	3 Monts
8	Castelain Blond Bière
9	Jenlain Ambrée
10	Gavroche

Germany

1	Andechser Doppelbock Dunkel
2	Ayinger Celebrator Doppelbock
3	Schneider Aventinus
4	Aecht Schlenkerla Fastenbier
5	Weltenburger Kloster Asam Bock
6	Schneider Aventinus Weizen-Eisbock
7	Kulmbacher Eisbock
8	Aecht Schlenkerla Rauchbier Urbock
9	Bürgerbräu Wolnzacher Hell
10	Neuzeller Kloster-Bräu Porter

Netherlands

1	La Trappe Quadrupel
2	t IJ Struis
3	De Hemel Nieuw Ligt Grand Cru
4	t IJ IJnde Jaars
5	La Trappe Tripel
6	Christoffel Blond
7	t IJ Zatte
8	La Trappe Dubbel

9	Scheldebrouwerij Hansje Drinker
10	Mestreechs Aajt

Poland

1	Apis Póltorak Jadwiga Mead
2	Zywiec Porter
3	Apis Dwojniak Kurpiowski
4	Lednicki Miód
5	Black Boss Porter
6	Kasztelanski Miód Trójniak
7	Amber Kozlak
8	Namyslow Zamkowe Mocne
9	Elbrewery Hevelius Kaper
10	Namyslow Rycerskie (Knight) Mocne

Scotland

1	Traquair Jacobite Ale
2	Traquair House Ale
3	Harviestoun Old Engine Oil
4	Belhaven Wee Heavy
5	Orkney Skullsplitter
6	Harviestoun Old Engine Oil Special Reserve
7	McEwans Scotch Ale
8	Harviestoun Bitter & Twisted (Cask)
9	Broughton Old Jock Ale
10	Orkney Dark Island

Sweden

1	Nynäshamns Fatlagrad Smörpundet Porter
2	Ahlafors Kåtisbock
3	Nils Oscar Imperial Stout
4	Slottskällans Imperial Stout
5	Nynäshamns Pickla Pils
6	Carnegie Porter
7	Nynäshamns Mysingen Midvinterbrygd
8	Jämtlands Oatmeal Porter

9   Nils Oscar Kalasöl
10   Jämtlands Postiljon

USA
1   Three Floyds Dark Lord Russian Imperial Stout
2   Bells Expedition Stout
3   Kuhnhenn Raspberry Eisbock
4   AleSmith Speedway Stout
5   Three Floyds Dreadnaught Imperial IPA
6   Stone Imperial Russian Stout
7   Oggis Hop Whompus
8   AleSmith Barrel Aged Old Numbskull
9   AleSmith YuleSmith India Pale Ale
10   Founders Breakfast Stout

THE AUSTRALIAN INTERNATIONAL BEER AWARDS

The Australian International Beer Awards (AIBA), founded in 1993 and held in Melbourne, is the third largest brewing event in the world. Its 2005 competition attracted 885 entries from 30 countries to be judged by an expert panel in numerous different classes. Most valued of all are the Championship Trophies, of which there are 12, one of which is for packaging and most but not all of which have outside sponsors. The 11 beer-related trophies for the 2005 competition were:

Highest Scoring Beer
Grand Champion Trophy
Doryman's Dark Ale
(Pelican Pub & Brewery, Oregon, USA)

Best Victorian Beer
Premier's Trophy
Supershine and Supershine Vintage
(Grand Bridge Brewery, Victoria)

Champion Australasian Brewery
University of Ballarat Vice-Chancellor's Trophy
South Australian Brewing Company

Champion International Brewery
International Malting Company Trophy
Pelican Pub & Brewery, Oregon, USA

Champion Small Brewery
Australian Enological Brewing Services Trophy
Founders Organic Brewery, New Zealand

Champion Specialty Beer
National Liquor News Trophy
Weihenstephan Hefeweissbier
(Weihenstephan Brewery, Germany)

Champion Lager
Visy Industries Trophy
Bohemian Pilzner
(Matilda Bay Brewing Company, Australia)

Champion Ale
Lancer Pacific Trophy
Doryman's Dark Ale
(Pelican Pub & Brewery, Oregon, USA)

Champion Stout
Coopers Best Extra Stout
(Coopers Brewery, South Australia)

Champion Porter
Samuel Adams Holiday Porter
(Boston Beer Company, USA)

Champion Reduced Alcohol Beer
City of Ballarat Trophy
Hahn Premium Light
(Swan Brewery Company, Western Australia)

*"Hath thy ale virtue, or thy beer strength, that the tongue
of man may be tickled, and his palate pleased in the morning?"*
Ben Jonson

The CAMRA Awards

The Campaign for Real Ale presents its awards annually at the Great British Beer Festival. Awards are presented in a number of categories, with an overall winner proclaimed the Champion Beer of Britain. The 2005 CAMRA Awards (with runners-up) were as follows:

Mild Category
Gold
Grainstore Rutland Panther
Silver
Brains' Dark
Bronze
Elgood's Black Dog

Bitter Category
Gold
Woodforde's Wherry
Silver
Holdens Black Country Bitter
Bronze (tie)
RCH PG Steam
Belvoir Star

Best Bitter Category
Gold
Harveys Sussex Bitter
Silver
Mighty Oak Burntwood Bitter
Bronze (tie)
Timothy Taylor Landlord
Olde Swan Entire

Golden Ales Category
Gold
Crouch Vale Brewers Gold
Silver
Jarrow Rivet Catcher
Bronze
Oakham JHB

Strong Ale Category
Gold
Hanby Nutcracker
Silver
Bullmastiff Son of a Bitch
Bronze
Fullers ESB

Speciality Category
Gold
Cairngorm Tradewinds
Silver
Young's Waggledance
Bronze (tie)
Daleside Morocco
Ridleys Rumpus

Real Ale in a Bottle Category
Gold
Durham Evensong
Silver
Young's Special London Ale
Bronze
Titanic Stout

Champion Beer of Britain
Gold
Crouch Vale Brewers Gold
Silver
Grainstore Rutland Panther
Bronze
Woodforde's Wherry